To Brian
Have a good read.

SECRET LOVE

Love -
Nan -

Feb. 14. 2000

SECRET LOVE

MY LIFE WITH FATHER MICHAEL CLEARY

PHYLLIS HAMILTON

WITH
PAUL WILLIAMS

MAINSTREAM
PUBLISHING

EDINBURGH AND LONDON

First published in Great Britain in 1995 by
MAINSTREAM PUBLISHING COMPANY (EDINBURGH) LTD
7 Albany Street
Edinburgh EH1 3UG

ISBN 1 85158 814 0

A catalogue record for this book is available from the British Library

Typeset in Palatino
Printed and bound in Great Britain by Butler and Tanner Ltd, Frome

Photo credits:
Unless credited otherwise all the photographs are copyright *Sunday World* and are reproduced with their permission. The photograph of Phyllis Hamilton and Ross Hamilton is by Val Sheehan of *Sunday World*.

CONTENTS

ACKNOWLEDGEMENTS

WHEN I FINALLY decided to tell the story of my life with Father Michael Cleary I was terrified for both our son Ross and for myself. I had shunned the outside world for so long that I was in completely uncharted waters. But my determination that my son would no longer have to be afraid or ashamed of who he was, spurred me on. But I simply would not have been able to get this far were it not for the help, support and trust of a small number of dedicated friends, family and professionals.

My thanks to my lawyers, Peter Lennon and Douglas Heather for the respect and understanding they showed to Ross and me at a time when we needed it most. My thanks also to Hugh Mohan, B.L. who has worked hard on my behalf.

My deepest thanks goes to *Sunday World* journalist Paul Williams and his editor Colm MacGinty. They worked hard to tell the world my story. I also wish to express my gratitude to Paul Williams for the long hours of hard work and his patience in putting this book together for me.

My gratitude also goes to Professor Ivor Browne, my doctor and friend, who probably risked more than anyone else in his willingness to stand by us when others wouldn't or couldn't. He watched over us with concern for many years and promised that when the time came he would speak out. It took a lot of courage.

My thanks to my family for their constant moral support and their patience with me for my lack of action and indecision for 18 months.

My heartfelt gratitude to Suzanne and her family for her constant companionship to both Ross and myself. She supported us through thick and thin even at the expense of her own freedom. Also to James who helped look after the house and garden to enable us to retain our dignity. And to Eileen for her letters of encouragement and being a champion of the truth.

And lastly to my son Ross for his love.

INTRODUCTION

IT HAD BEEN a pleasant evening sitting in the front room of Michael Cleary's house in Marino watching TV, drinking tea and talking about nothing in particular. It had been six weeks or so since I met this warm, friendly priest. For the first time in my life I had begun to feel rather special. No one had ever listened to the story of my miserable life with the same understanding and compassion as Michael Cleary.

I was a confused, troubled kid of 17. My life had been a traumatic, depressing mess over which I had absolutely no control. Violence, sex abuse and poverty were the hallmarks of my early life growing up in a broken home. Then there were the orphanages, where beatings were dispensed in place of a family's love. From there it was on to a psychiatric hospital full of tortured hearts and minds. I had been a slave to circumstance from the moment of my conception. I had always been surrounded by an impenetrable wall which confined my spirit, stultified my growth as a person. Michael Cleary punched the first hole in that wall, letting in a ray of sunlight to my dark world.

Michael was twice my age and I looked up to him as a deeply knowledgeable man. Since our first encounter he had made me feel safe and secure in his company. I wasn't afraid of being abused or hurt while with him. He tried to give me confidence in myself, made me feel that I was an important person in my own right. I had something to say the same as everyone else and therefore deserved the respect of being heard.

On this particular evening Michael and I were alone together in the house. It was unusual because there were always so many people coming and going. There was a lot of happiness whenever he was around. Michael's exuberant personality could light up a room the moment he walked into it. He was so tall (six feet four inches!) and distinguished looking you couldn't miss him. But tonight he appeared to be different, more warm and affectionate than usual. He sat in the armchair next to mine looking into my eyes with a smile that I would grow to recognise over the next 26 years. It unsettled me a little but at the same time I loved the attention. I was the most important person in the world at that moment. Around 9 p.m. I decided that it was time to go back to St Brendan's where I was working as an auxiliary nurse. I put on my coat and Michael walked me to the front door.

In the hallway he stepped ahead of me as if to open the front door. Instead he turned around and bent his head down close to mine. He caught my arms with his big strong hands and kissed me on the lips. It was a kiss like no other. Before this Michael had always kissed me gently on the cheek and given me a reassuring friendly hug whenever I called. He would do the same again when I was leaving. But this was completely different and it frightened me. His lips were firm and moist as they forced mine apart. I tried to keep them shut but felt powerless to resist. He was breathing heavily, it was almost as if he was panting. There was an urgency in his action which I didn't understand. I could smell the cigarette smoke on his breath and his clothes. I was totally confused. My mind was racing. Part of me wanted to pull away and run, run for my life. The other told me to stay.

The kiss seemed to last forever. He could feel my body

trembling and pulled me into his chest. The top of my head just about reached his chest. Compared to my petite frame he was a monster. I could just about hear his heart pounding excitedly over the thumping of my own. My mouth was dry. He rubbed my long hair and calmed me down a little. Then he cupped my head in his hands and looked into my face. He lowered his voice to a gentle whisper.

'Phyl, I think you a very beautiful young woman, I have done since I first set eyes on you . . . I love you.' His words stunned me. I couldn't speak. I didn't know what to say. Michael could see the fear and confusion in my eyes and put his arm around me. We walked back into the sitting-room together. He sat me on his knee and again kissed me on the lips. This time it was softer and sweeter, he pushed his tongue between them and then kissed my face, my eyes, my neck. His hands explored my body, touching me in a way that no one had ever done before. I was still nervous but felt strangely comfortable in his arms.

Michael stopped kissing me and held my hands in his. Then he suggested that we exchange marriage vows so that we could be 'man and wife in the eyes of God'. I think I blurted out something like, 'But you are a priest – we can't get married'. As soon as I said those words I regretted them. I wanted to be the wife of a man so special. I felt suddenly reckless. Then he smiled reassuringly. 'In the days before Jesus there was no marriage ceremony so a man and woman simply exchanged vows between them and they were married,' he told me. So we exchanged vows.

I sat in one chair and Michael beside me in another, holding my hands and looking into my eyes. 'Phyllis McDaid, I Michael Cleary, take you to be my lawfully wedded wife, to have and to hold from this day forward till death do us part.' Then it was my turn, I was so nervous and excited that I stuttered through the words. 'Michael Cleary, I Phyllis McDaid take you to be my lawfully wedded hu . . . husband, to have and to hold from this day forward, till death do us part.' I couldn't believe what I was hearing myself say. I was overwhelmed with a sense of joy. I began to cry, but for the first time in my life they were tears of happiness. I hugged Michael and we both kissed.

It was then that I heard the word 'consummation' for the first time. Michael explained that to be truly married in the eyes of God the marriage had to be consummated. This, he explained like a teacher, meant having 'full penetrative sex or sexual intercourse'. I had no idea what was going on. Sex or relationships were never mentioned when you were being reared by the nuns and modesty was hammered into you. When I asked him what that meant Michael smiled and described the sex act. It scared me because I began remembering what my father had done to me as a little girl. Then Michael told me to watch and he would demonstrate what happened when a man was aroused. He began masturbating in front of me. I was dumbfounded. When he had finished I wondered to myself why there was so much nonsense and fear about sex. It also dawned on me that this was just normal behaviour between people who loved each other.

Michael said that we would consummate the relationship when I came back. There was no forcefulness or pressure but he made it understood that in order for us to be truly married we had to make love. But he warned me that we could only share our love for one another in secret. No one could know that we were married. 'As long as God knows that is all that matters,' he told me as he again saw me to the front door. I caught a bus back to St Brendan's that night. I couldn't stop smiling and had to restrain myself from telling the world my wonderful news. I was married to the most wonderful man in the world. I couldn't sleep a wink that night. And that was the start of a forbidden secret love affair which would last 26 years until Michael's death on New Year's Eve 1993.

It was never meant to be a normal relationship. It couldn't have been. To the outside world Michael Cleary was the dedicated, charismatic singing priest. He was a caring, loving man who helped anyone who came to him for assistance or advice. To the outside world I became his housekeeper and secretary who helped run his busy life. But behind the presbytery doors we were lovers, parents, husband and wife.

Living a lie took a terrible toll on our lives and we paid a high price for our love. Ostensibly, Michael had no problem living a double life, but I had dreadful difficulty with it. We had two children together. One was put up for adoption, the other, Ross, we reared together. I was always prepared to take our secret to the grave but circumstances which have occurred since his death over 21 months ago have forced me into the public arena . . . the last place in the world Ross or I wanted to find ourselves.

In June 1995 we told the world our story through the *Sunday World* newspaper. It took an extraordinary amount of soul-searching to do that. It was terrifying, but it was the only course of action open to us. We did so in order that we would never again feel the need to hide or be afraid. We were praised and supported by a great many good people for our courage. But we also suffered the hate and castigation of others. At least my story is no longer an unmentionable scandal.

Before his death Michael hoped and trusted that his secret family would be cared for. Unfortunately, that never happened and we were left with nothing. Through the media our life with Michael was denied by those who refused to accept that the priest they placed on a pedestal was also a man, someone with all the idiosyncrasies and traits of any normal person. It had a particularly upsetting effect on our son. We suffered our pain and our grief in silence until we could no longer carry that burden.

I made the decision to write this book to put the record straight and end a nightmare that has gone on for almost two years. No matter how unpalatable it is to certain groups, it is the truth and the truth cannot be altered. It is a story filled with sadness and heartache. Writing it has been painful but it has also served as a cleansing period in my life. I want to use this as an opportunity to leave the past behind and start afresh. Through its telling I can forgive those who have chosen to distance themselves from us during those long months of anguish and rejection. But it is not a bitter diatribe. I have not set out to hurt or embarrass anyone and that is why I have decided not to name or accuse a lot of people. Revenge is a sinful waste of human strength.

I also hope that in some way it can be a source of consolation for all those anonymous women and priests in Ireland today who have been driven to secrecy by an uncaring Church which continues to impose a cruel precept called celibacy. An organisation which forbids its disciples to be ministers as well as husbands and fathers, to enjoy the God-given right of companionship and love.

This book is the story of my life with Father Michael Cleary.

Phyl Hamilton,
September 1995

CHAPTER ONE

The Unwanted Child

MY TROUBLES STARTED before the day I was even born. In fact I was never meant to be born. Firstly, my mother couldn't cope with any more children. She already had three in a row and more than had her hands full trying to rear children all under the age of three. It probably wouldn't have been so bad if our home had been a happy place but happiness was a very scarce commodity. My mother and father were like chalk and cheese. They were caught in a loveless, bitter relationship. And in such cases it is the children who suffer, finding themselves sandwiched in the middle. He was a gambler and drinker and she was a staunch Catholic. Very often there wasn't enough money to buy clothes and food. And he took out his frustration and anger by ramming his big fists into my mother's jaw. I was the last thing in the world either of them wanted.

After the first three children were born in quick succession, doctors in the maternity hospital sewed up her womb in the hope that she could have no more. In the days of no contraception it was the only thing that could be done to prevent more babies. However, she did conceive again and almost died in labour at the age of 28. Because of the way I was confined in the womb her doctors thought I would be stillborn or deformed in some way. On 28 February 1950 they had to hold my mother down during emergency surgery and ripped her open while she was still in her senses, in order to save both our lives. She was in such excruciating pain that she actually begged them to cut her to end the agony. We survived and my life began.

I was christened in a church on Aughrim Street and was looked after by an aunt for the first six months of my life in order to allow my mother to recover from her ordeal. Throughout my life my mother always reminded me about the agony she suffered giving birth to me, which gave me a guilt complex. I had brought no joy into the world and simply wasn't wanted. In the subsequent years my mother would give birth to three more children – in all there were six girls and one boy – all of whom at one time were under 13 years of age.

We lived in a rented semi-detached, three-bedroomed house on the North Circular Road in Dublin. My mother was Philomena Gaffney from Palmerstown. She was an attractive woman with blonde hair and blue eyes. Everyone said that I looked very much like her and there were times that I had good reason for resenting that. Born in 1922 she was the youngest of eleven children and was spoiled by her mother and siblings. She couldn't cope with the extraordinary demands of rearing so many little children at the same time with little physical or financial support from her husband. She vented her frustrations by beating us. Upon reflection, that was all the poor woman could do to relieve the pent-up anger and stultified emotions. In those days, being a wife and mother was the role expected of the average woman living in a Catholic, male-dominated Ireland. She was, effectively, a prisoner of circumstance.

Shortly before I was born she went to see a priest and told him that she could not go on living the way she was, producing children in poverty while at the same time incurring regular beatings from her husband. A priest was the only person she thought she could get advice from. Instead, she was severely admonished. He told her to go home to her husband and children. She had made her bed and she had better lie in it. Those harsh, unfeeling words must have dealt a terrible blow to her flagging morale. Effectively, he was telling her she was a prisoner of circumstance and there was very little light at the end of the tunnel.

I was once told that before she met my father, she had been in love with a much-older man and wanted to marry him. But my grandmother forbade the relationship and split them up. I am convinced she married my father on the rebound. She also did it to spite grandmother because he was in the Irish army and marrying a soldier was frowned upon.

He was Brendan McDaid from County Tyrone. Born just after the First World War in 1918 he was a fine big man well over six feet in height and resembled Clark Gable in looks and build. He had a thick head of jet black hair, brown eyes and a moustache. When he was eleven his mother and father split up and went their separate ways leaving him in the care of his grandparents in Dundalk, County Louth. As a child my mother told me he had been a carrier of scarlet fever which made him immune to the effects of the disease but resulted in killing his grandparents. After that he was moved around between aunts and uncles. He had a very unhappy childhood.

When he was 14 years of age he ran away to join the army. He was tired of being passed around by his relatives. He forged his birth certificate and got into the ranks. He never had much love or affection in his life and didn't know how to show it to his wife or his children. He was a very hurt individual. The years before 16 are the most important in the development of an individual. The cold, hard disciplinary life of a soldier has no place for the sensitivities of a developing teenage boy. He retired from the army when I was still very young because he was suffering with osteo-arthritis in his hands. He got a job in the Customs House for a while and then became unemployed like tens of thousands of others in the dark days of economic depression of the 1950s.

There were always rows in our house in the few years I was living there. They always seemed to be at each other's throats. The rows frightened me and my brother and sisters. My father drank and gambled practically every penny we owned. He would come in drunk and beat my mother senseless. Mother absolutely detested alcohol all her life. My earliest memory of those fights was when I was around four years old. I was standing at the top of the stairs listening to them argue about something. I hated the sounds of them fighting, especially the angry growling voice of my father as he hurled obscenities. Then he began throttling her and almost strangled her. When you are a small little child everything appears much more terrifying. I shivered with fear and thought to myself, 'Oh God, Daddy was going to kill my Mammy'. Another time he broke her teeth with a punch and she had to get them all extracted and replaced with dentures.

But there were times that I felt she was hard on him too. Once he came home laden with food. All of us were hungry because there was nothing to eat. We couldn't believe our eyes. He was smiling and all happy with himself. He told my mother that he had placed all his money on a horse which won a race and tripled his cash. She screamed abuse at him for being so recklessly irresponsible, risking starvation on one horse. 'What would we have done if the damn horse fell at the last fence?' I remember her words so clearly. But all we were thinking was 'Will you wait until we have eaten before you have a row . . . we're famished.'

Regularly we went to school without any breakfast and came home to no food. But I was very proud and wouldn't tell anyone. One day a teacher called me up to her desk in school and asked what I would eat when I got home. I told her that I was going to have carrots, chicken, gravy, potatoes and a big dessert. But the food was a fantasy in my proud little head. Then she picked up a sandwich and a piece of cake she had left over from her own lunch and gave it to another kid. I learned my lesson the hard way about pride. I watched someone else eating what I should have been eating. Pride doesn't relieve the hunger pains in your stomach.

There were many nights when my father didn't come home. My mother would say that he was off with other women. Being such a good-looking man he had women dripping off him. But the other women failed to quench his appetite for sex. From as far back as I can recall he and my mother slept in separate beds. It is quite possible that the only times they slept together she conceived because I have no recollection of any affection between them. That was the reason I believe he began sexually abusing me.

My most vivid memory of the abuse was when I was around seven years old. I had been off from school with a cold. My mother was going out and somehow suggested I go into the back room where my father slept. I got into bed beside him and he began cradling me in his lap. I got frightened when I felt something hard between my legs. I didn't know what was happening but I sensed it was wrong. His arms were tight around me and suddenly there was a terrific pain, anal pain. I cried out 'You will go to hell' as I tried to break away from his grip. 'Not at all – you are my little girl,' he whispered into my ear. He warned me not to tell my mother about what happened. I can't recall how many times it happened after that, nor do I want to. Dredging up those nightmares is devastating. To this day I am certain I have never fully dealt with the trauma of the abuse. He never looked me in the face when he was interfering with me. It was always from behind. I know that I was the only one in the family he abused and I think it was because I looked so much like my mother. I resented her for that and the fact that if she had slept with him maybe he would have left me alone.

But I was helpless to do anything about it because there was no one to tell. The abuse didn't take place on a regular basis but I lived in fear of him doing it to me. I was terrified of being on my own with him, even after I grew up. At night when I went to bed I was too scared to sleep. I would wait until the others in the room were asleep and then get out through the window and hide behind the garden shed. I watched for the light to go out in his room before creeping back into the room and bed. I was so terrified of the abuse that I endured my fear of the bats which swirled around in the dark above my head. I also subdued my fear about the ghosts and banshees coming out of the bushes to get me.

I learned to live with it and cried alone in my sleep. It is a trauma which never goes away. It lurks hidden away in the back of the victim's mind, occasionally emerging to wreak havoc in the head, before retreating to the recesses of the memory. As a result of the abuse I never really enjoyed sex and could have happily lived without it in my life. In fact, even with Michael I often clammed up when it came to sex. Years later, when Michael revealed to a relative that he was Ross's father, I was told: 'If you were sexually abused as a child you had to have been more experienced than Michael.' If only that person knew the reality. In a strange way my father had a softness my mother did not possess. I had always intended to confront the issue and ask him why, but he died before I got that opportunity.

By the time I was five years of age all seven of us were in and out of orphanages so often it made our heads spin. Each time our parents split up and there wasn't enough money to care for us the social workers came and took us away. At first I used to cry, but then I got used to it, like it was somehow normal. When our parents made up we were dragged home, only to be sent back again. It caused confusion, instability and overwhelming insecurity in all of us. I often wished that I was an orphan and I wouldn't have to go home to either of them. I hated them.

Before I was nine years old I had been in and out of the orphanage at Goldenbridge in Inchicore at least five times. It was a big austere-looking place and I hated it. It was run by overworked, but well-meaning nuns. Symbolically, it was demolished some years later with the emergence of a more enlightened era. At the height of the appalling economic misery of the 1950s children from broken homes who were in need of care were dumped in the orphanages, which were run by religious orders, because they were the only places where the health authorities could put kids. And there were a lot of children like us. Unemployment and poverty among those who did not opt for the boat to England were the major factors which contributed to family breakdowns in post-war Ireland. When you came from a broken home the system discriminated against you. You were beaten and abused at home and then beaten again in the orphanage. Love and attention were not on the curriculum in this harsh education. It was hard for a youngster to keep his or her sanity amid such confusion and hurt. The State was happy to abdicate its responsibilities and leave the donkey work to the institutions of the Church.

The orphanage was crammed full of sad, lonely children who wanted to be loved. Everyone was given a number, mine was 103 during one of my terms there. The ages ranged from babies only a few months old to 16, the official age for termination of care. Some of the carers had been inmates themselves and had stayed on to help the nuns and also because they probably had nowhere else to go.

Our day would start at 6 a.m. with Mass and then breakfast. After breakfast we had chores to do and then it was school. After school we had more chores and were then put to making rosary beads. At 5.45 p.m. every evening we all had to kneel, one behind the other, in a line along the corridor outside the dining hall which seemed to go on forever it was so long. One of the nuns would recite the Angelus before supper. Afterwards it was more chores, the rosary and then bed. We slept in big dormitories. During the winter nights it would be so cold that I couldn't sleep until my body's need for rest overcame its need for warmth. We were starving from supper until breakfast because we had to fast from the night before if we were going to Mass. We had no choice in the matter.

Bedtime was at 9 p.m. If you had been caught for some infraction of the very many, stringent rules, you were rounded up for punishment. It was when you were most vulnerable, shivering in your night-dress. I would stand there in the corridor outside the dormitory with my back against the wall listening to the crack of the cane. I would say to myself, 'I will not cry' over and over. Once you cried the beating ended. But I stubbornly refused to cry until I got under the cover on my bed. Then the tears would flow long after I had fallen asleep.

One of the most awful things was that you only got one change of clothes and underwear a week. At night it was checked to see if it was dirty before going to bed. You were beaten if it was. We had a bath once every two weeks and the same water was used for 10 or 15 girls, so there was always a rush at bath time to be first in. At 7 a.m. on Sunday mornings we were all marched off for Mass to the local church. We would attend two Masses and then go for breakfast. Unlike today, Sunday Mass lasted a full hour. Then all the children were marched back for a third and maybe a fourth Mass of the morning. We weren't allowed go to the toilet during these marathon church sessions. You'd almost have to crawl along the floor before they'd let you go. One morning I wasn't allowed to go. During the Mass I went in my pants. I was no more than six years of age and couldn't hold it any longer. All the other girls looked at me. I was terrified. During breakfast one of the carer/teachers made an example of me in front of everyone else. I was called a 'filthy, dirty little brat to do such a thing in Holy God's church'. Then I was dragged out and cleaned up.

When I was nine I was taken from my family into care to the orphanage at St Anne's in Booterstown. I never lived with my family again after that. I was glad, because I couldn't take the abuse, the rows or the instability anymore. At least I was going to be in the one place all the time. I have good memories of that place even though it was very strict and sometimes harsh. There were about 100 of us so the nuns and carers were not overwhelmed by the numbers. My number was 97. We got into all kinds of mischief. I made friends with a girl who was also called Phyllis. She was really wild and full of fun. One day she asked me to run away with her. I don't remember how far we got before being caught. We were both punished. The next day Phyllis was taken out of her class and shifted to another home in Moate. She had been a regular absconder and the nuns reckoned it was the only place to put her. She was separated from her sisters, who were also in Booterstown, and never seen again. I was very sad but reckoned that if I kept running away that I, too, would be sent to Moate and then I would never have to go home to my feuding parents again. In my childish innocence I thought that they would never find me in such a far-flung place. I had no idea that Ireland was such a small country.

So running away became a pattern for me as I grew older. Every chance I got I was out through the gates and on my way; each time I took someone with me. I always ensured I had matches or money to buy matches so that I could light a fire in case I got cold. The others used to call me 'the little match girl'. But we never got to stay away overnight. On one of those adventures I ran away with two girls called May and Joan. We walked into the city centre. May met a woman she knew and told her that we had run away from the orphanage. She made up some story about cruelty and abuse to convince the woman to help us. She was sympathetic and gave us some money to catch a bus.

We took a bus somewhere out of town and then began walking silently through fields. May was leading the way and I had no idea where we were headed. It was exciting because I had never been into what I considered to be the country before. Then we came upon a gypsy camp. The big old gypsy caravans were parked in a circle around a large roaring fire with beautiful golden flames curling up and vanishing in the air. Their horses grazed nearby. Bold as brass, May just walked up and began warming herself at the crackling fire. We stood beside her. The heat was comforting.

An old white-haired woman wrapped in a shawl looked at us before disappearing into one of the caravans. There didn't seem to be anyone else around. A few minutes later a tall man in a well-worn coat and leather boots appeared at the door. He looked old, with a weather-beaten, wrinkled face and long-flowing snow-white hair draped across his shoulders. He looked like someone out of a fairy-tale story. He stared across the flames into my eyes and pointed his finger. 'You, the good-looking one, come over here,' he suddenly demanded in a strange croaking voice.

I was terrified and a shiver went down my spine. Joan and I took to our heels and ran for our lives. When we got to the end of the field we discovered that May was missing. We looked around and saw her still staring, mesmerised, into the golden, hypnotic flames. We screamed out her name and she turned and came running to catch up. Other gypsies began appearing and came running after us. We jumped into a garden and lay flat on our stomachs hardly breathing while we heard the gypsies looking for us. We stayed there until they had gone.

What had begun as an adventure was now a nightmare. We were paranoid and frightened. We walked on along the road until we saw a policeman. We began running in the opposite direction and he came after us. We jumped into another garden and tried to hide but he caught Joan and me. May had got away but came back when she saw that we'd been caught. The policeman knocked at a house and phoned for a squad car to pick us up. He asked us what had happened and where we were from but we would tell him nothing. He was a nice man and we eventually told him. When the police car arrived he instructed someone on the radio to call the orphanage. The three of us gulped and looked at each other. We were going to get it this time. He kept us until the nuns arrived in a taxi to collect us. I was put sitting in the back seat wedged between the two nuns. They took turns in whacking me all the way back to Booterstown.

Despite the punishment I kept running off. One day I and another girl sneaked off to see a movie in Dun Laoire. It was the Elvis Presley picture, *It Happened at the World's Fair*. As we settled into our seats I got the shock of my life when I spotted my mother, sitting two rows down on her own. My heart missed a beat and I hunched down further in case she saw me. I don't know which I watched more, the movie or my mother. As the credits rolled she left, none the wiser that I was there. That night we got into an unlocked car and slept in it. The next morning we stole a bottle of milk from a doorstep and shared it for breakfast. Later that day we gave up and decided to go back.

Sister Lagori was one of the nuns I liked most in St Anne's. She was an excellent teacher and I learned a lot from her. She once told me that she became a nun to get away from her family of 16 brothers and sisters. She often laughed about how she got away from children only to be put looking after children. She was very understanding towards kids. She had a philosophical expression which she often repeated, 'Never judge a flower until it is fully grown'. After the trip to the cinema she took me aside to talk with me. She was concerned about my reasons for always running away. I told her that it was because I wanted to be put down the country where my parents couldn't get me, especially my father. I had no words to express what I was trying to say. Then she asked me: 'Was he interfering with you child?' In a flood of tears I told her the whole story. It was like she had turned a key to my heart and all the pain and anguish came gushing out. In a way I was relieved that at last I told someone about it. After that I was sent a few times for psychological help, but while I was asked a lot of questions no one seemed to listen to the answers. Nothing else was ever done about it except that I did not have to go home any more.

In general the food was very average although adequate.

There was little room for variety. Our meals consisted of porridge, bread and butter, and cocoa, which we called dish-water, for breakfast. Lunch was normally minced meat with cabbage and potatoes on weekdays, and sausages and peas on Sundays with rice pudding and semolina for dessert. The problem with the food, though, was that there were 14 hours every day when we didn't get any because we were fasting before Mass. I could never get used to fasting. I was so frail that I used to faint a lot if I hadn't eaten. We had nothing to eat from 6 p.m. until 8 a.m. The other girls used to tease me about fainting, saying that everyone could see my knickers when I passed out.

One morning I collapsed during morning Mass. Later, the priest, a big, fearsome man with a deep booming voice which sent shivers down the spine, came into my classroom. He stood at the top of the room and pointed at me. 'You, yes you cabbage head, stand up.' I stood there shivering in my shoes wondering what I had done wrong. 'Don't you ever come into Mass again without your breakfast,' he boomed before walking out of the room. Although the words sounded harsh they were music to my ears. Afterwards the nuns allowed me to stay in bed while everyone else was at Mass. I was transferred to Our Lady's dormitory to look after the little ones who didn't have to go to Mass. We used to have great fun there at night when the nuns had gone to bed. We would pull mattresses onto the floor and do all kinds of gymnastics. We also used to make sure that the younger children had gone to the toilet before getting into bed in case they wet themselves during the night. Bedwetters were often openly castigated in front of everyone else.

I began to make the most of my life in the orphanage. As kids from traumatic backgrounds our only form of escape was to make our own fun whenever the opportunity arose. At that time there were a lot of fears that, following the vision in Fatima, the world was going to end. I had a special, secret place in my mind where I could go when things were becoming too much for me. I used to tell the other kids that I had this special place under the sea where I would be safe. If any of them wanted to come with me then they would have to pay. I had a price list of sweets and money in return for securing a safe place in my secret world under the sea. That was where I got the money to go to the cinema. Medical missionaries from down the road used to come up to St Anne's for devotions. When they were inside we would 'borrow' their bikes and cycle down to Blackrock to catch part of a picture and have the bikes back in time for them coming out without noticing a thing.

We were all in the choir where most of the songs we sang were in Latin. Most of the time we didn't know the words and just made up our own which was quite funny . . . until you were caught. The punishment was to have your hair cut short. I had mine cut a few times. There was a doddery old nun, Sr. Augusta, who was always after us. She was a nice old dear whose role in life, it appeared, was shouting at us to stop doing what we were doing and to do something else. She had taken on herself the job of glorified orphanage policewoman. In the grounds outside there was an apple orchard. There was one special tree which had the nicest apples of all but Sr. Augusta had a goal in life not to let us near it. We jokingly called it 'Adam's tree' and every chance we got we were pulling apples from it. She was always chasing us out of it and giving off. Adam's tree was the death of the poor woman. One day she got a heart attack chasing someone.

When I first went to St Anne's the Reverend Mother was Sr. Thomasina, a lovely quiet, gentle soul. She had a twitch in her eye and whenever I saw her twitching I always winked back because I thought she liked me and was winking at me. I felt like a proper fool when one of the girls explained the situation to me. She gave me and another girl the job of cleaning up the convent. At the end of each week she paid us both with a bag of sweets, a Crunchie and a half-crown. People used to bring loads of sweets and cakes for the orphanage but the kids rarely saw them. They were stored in a great big cabinet in the parlour. When no one was looking I would stuff big handfuls of them down the front of my pink pinafore which was the uniform we wore. Other times I would bring a wastepaper basket and fill it up with bars and then cover it over with a duster. Outside I would share them with my friends. I was their version of Robin Hood. I was very sad the day Sr. Thomasina died and I didn't much like her successor. I kept on the cleaning chores but there was no more payment. But at least I still had access to the treasure in the closet which more than compensated.

One of the hardest chores we had to do was washing the clothes in the old laundry. Winter was worst of all. We used to wash the clothes in big wooden troughs with brass taps. They would soak over the weekend and on Monday mornings and afternoons we would have to break the icy water to wring out the garments. It was a miracle we didn't get frostbite. Then we would scrub them on washboards.

My friends and I were often used by the older girls to do their mischief, because we were considered to be the wild girls. Across the field was a big storehouse. One evening one of the bigger girls told us she had seen a lorry load of tinned fruit being delivered to the storehouse and asked us to go and get some. We got out by the fire escape when everyone was in bed. There were dogs on guard outside where the fruit was kept but they knew us and didn't bark. We got five tins each and pierced them on the spikes of the gates. Before the end of the week practically every kid in the orphanage had raided the storehouse and there were empty tins everywhere. When the nuns found out there was absolute war. Everyone was lined up, especially the main culprits, my friends and I. We all had our heads in our hands which convinced the nuns that we were crying when in fact we were laughing. We all got a few slaps and were ordered to pay two shillings each in compensation.

As the years went by the number of children in St Anne's gradually reduced and with that life became easier. With Sr.

Lagori I began to love school. In June 1963 I did my primary cert, as it was known, and passed with flying colours. It was also the day I became a woman – I had my first menstrual cycle. At first I was terrified at the sight of so much blood. A nun handed me a brown paper package and I was told that 'This will probably happen every month for the rest of your life'. On the landing of the Sacred Heart dormitory was a locked closet. We had often wondered what was kept in there under lock and key. The bigger girls would regularly open it and carry out a big box to the incinerator. Now there was no more mystery – and very little explanation either. I went through hell during puberty. I was terrified by the transformation my body was going through because we were never taught about puberty and development. I was embarrassed and I felt like a freak.

There was greater emphasis too on games and music. We entertained ourselves by putting on pageants. One Christmas we all got roller-skates and performed plays on them in the recreation hall. But there was a stop put to that when one of the girls crashed into a wall and broke her arm. The skates were confiscated. During the long winter nights we learned Irish dancing and ballet. We also did ballroom dancing which I enjoyed most. A husband and wife team called the Jeanettes came in to teach us. Just before class one evening, around 6 p.m. I discovered that there were a couple of buttons missing on my blouse. The nuns and carers had drummed it into us to be particular about our clothes and appearance. If your clothes were torn or dirty you were beaten or given some other form of punishment. The nuns had to be strict about such things because there wasn't very much money to buy replacement uniforms. I got a needle and thread and went to hide in the toilets in the yard to stitch them back on. I was relieved when I had them sown back on because I had averted getting into trouble.

I put the needle in my mouth to hold it while I folded up the blouse. Something happened which made me stumble and

I accidentally swallowed it. I didn't know what to do and went into a panic. I went out and told one of my friends. 'Oh God, that will go right to your heart and you'll be dead,' she told me which scared the living daylights out of me. I had no choice but to tell the nuns. They went into a right flap. Sr. Augusta brought me into the teachers' room and started giving me cotton-wool sandwiches. If it hadn't been such an ordeal I might have found their remedy quite funny. I was rushed off to St Michael's hospital in Dun Laoire. I had never been in a hospital before and I was afraid of the doctors coming near me.

I didn't want the male doctor to examine me. I was scared of men because the only man I had ever known was my father. I thought every man was like him. Eventually I relented and let him carry out his examination. While I was lying on a bed in the casualty unit I said I wanted to go to the toilet. Instead I tried to run out of the place. The nurses stopped me and brought me back to the bed. Then they brought me a commode but I refused to use it. One of the carers gave me two shillings and said that I would be able to go home in a short while. I would just have to stay overnight and the next day would be able to go to see my sisters at home. As I got older I didn't mind going home for visits.

The next morning I was operated on to retrieve the needle. When I came around I was violently sick and jumping around the bed. The anaesthetic combined with a hefty portion of cotton-wool would have made an elephant sick. After a few days I was released from hospital. I was so delighted to get back to the orphanage. Up until then I hadn't really appreciated the place. It was a damn sight better place than hospital. But I wasn't to enjoy my new-found affection for St Anne's for long. It would be a pattern which has dogged my life. Everytime I began to enjoy a settled period other forces would disrupt the course of events. Heartache and upset were never far away.

CHAPTER TWO

The Nightmare

IF YOU WERE considered bright in Booterstown you were sent to secondary school on Haddington Road. It was a particularly good school and I was one of those sent there at the age of 13. I got friendly with twin sisters who came from a good home. I was from an orphanage and always told them that I had no mother or father. I was too ashamed to admit I had a family. Being accepted as an orphan kept things simple and avoided questions. I would go home on day visits but rarely stayed overnight. I told the twins that the woman who lived in our house was my aunt. I didn't want them to know that she was my mother. I liked being an orphan and it gave me a sense of security.

When I was 14 I went home for Hallowe'en to stay for the weekend. I was always nervous about going home because I didn't have much of a relationship with my mother and I was afraid that my father would interfere with me. She would hit me if I was late. Whenever I was in trouble in the orphanage the carers would call her. Then she would come to see me and beat me for causing trouble. I got off the bus a short distance from our house and began to cross the road. As I was crossing I dropped my rosary beads which I carried with me everywhere. As I bent down in the middle of the road to pick

31

them up I was hit by a motorbike and knocked to the ground. An ambulance took me off to the Mater Hospital. When I came to and realised what had happened I panicked because my mother would be wondering where I was. I ran out of the hospital before the nurses could stop me and went straight home. When I got in she was furious and didn't believe that I had been in an accident. She gave me a thumping and I went to bed feeling ill.

I was glad to get back to school the following Monday morning. At break time I felt sick and went to the toilet. I fainted in a cubicle. The twins found me lying in my own vomit on the ground. This time I didn't leave the hospital when I was brought in. An x-ray showed that I had concussion and delayed shock from the accident. I was kept there for a few weeks.

In the meantime, the twins, who knew the address of my 'aunt', called around to enquire how I was doing in hospital. My mother had no idea about my lies and when they called her my aunt she looked at them curiously and said she was my mother. My secret world of torment and shame was broken to the two people I most wanted to be friends with in the world. The twins came to see me in hospital and accused me of being a liar. I was in utter despair. I was completely crushed by their words.

From the moment I discovered that the twins knew my secret I wanted to die. It sparked off a chain reaction which exploded all the suppressed traumas I had endured during my 14 years of misery. Living in an imaginary world with no familial ties was my mental mechanism for pushing aside all the baggage of my past. Then I thought about the accident with the needle and how I had been told that it could go to my heart and I would die. So I reckoned that if I swallowed enough needles at least one of them would free me from my hell.

My recollection of what happened after that is blank. Things happened before I knew what was going on. I told a teacher something about my great plan for liberation. I suspect that the orphanage informed my mother of their fears that I was going to take my own life. I believe it was her who had me committed to a mental home. I was sedated and woke up in a bed in St Brendan's psychiatric hospital. It was like waking up into a nightmare. I had no idea where I was or even who I was. I was in a state of sheer terror and pulled the covers around me. I was in some sort of ward with five beds in it and a toilet on the far side. There were bars on the windows.

The movie *One Flew Over the Cuckoo's Nest* reminds me of that place. Across from me was an old lady, with wrinkled-up skin who was almost completely bald. She kept scratching her head with her long nails, rocking over and back with a blank, terrifying stare on her face. She looked a hundred years old. I jumped out of bed and ran to the toilet. Another woman with wild eyes stood over me and began slapping me across the face. I got past her and locked myself in the toilet until a nurse came and told me it was safe to come out.

When I got back into my bed another crazy woman put a pillow over my head and tried to smother me before the nurses pulled her away. I was out my mind with fear. Later, I was taken by the nurses to be weighed and medically examined. On the way down the stairs I fainted. Then I was transferred from the ward to a lock-up unit. It was even worse than the ward. There was every kind of mental illness and condition imaginable in that nightmarish place. There was one group of patients I called the psychos because they were literally very mad. They stole everything I had and hurled abuse at me. One of the names they called me was lesbian. I knew it must be some sort of insult even though I hadn't a clue what the word meant. I learned to survive in the place. It was like living in a jungle because there was no way out and danger seemed to lurk around every corner. I remember a doctor coming in to see me one day and telling me I shouldn't have been in there. He blamed the system because a mental hospital was the only place where traumatised kids like me could be treated.

You always had to be on guard in case you were suddenly attacked by one of the other patients. Anything was liable to happen. It was not unusual for someone to just get up and put her fists through the window or attack the nurses. I wanted to tell the staff that I was not mad like these other women and that I wanted to get out of the place, but no one seemed to hear me. The doctors had me on medication the same as everyone else in the place. When I was given pills I would hide them in my mouth and pretend to swallow. When no one was looking I would crush them into the floor.

After some time, I can't recall how long, I was transferred to St Loman's psychiatric home near Lucan. While I was there I had a run-in with a doctor and was sedated for a week. When I came to I vaguely recall my mother coming to see me. I was in a stupor and she slapped me across the face because I must have done something wrong. When I returned to a state I describe as normal, I decided to get out of there. I told another girl in the kitchens that I was going to run away and she said she would go with me. I arranged that when we got out we would meet in Booterstown Park. But when I left she told the nurses and they picked me up and brought me back. I was put to sleep for a few more days. In fact I don't blame either the nurses or the doctors for my treatment because that was the universally accepted practice in those days. Sedation was the panacea for all ills. If you had a bad day you were sedated. If you kicked up a fuss or argued, you were sedated.

It was around this time that I met Doctor Ivor Browne, a man who would become a lifelong friend and my crutch during times of crisis and emotional turmoil. He began therapy with me and reckoned that I was making progress. I was moved back to St Brendan's again where I began to enjoy what was referred to as liberty, which meant that I was free to move around the hospital and grounds and help the staff. I got friendly with this nun who was a patient. She was really nice and I could see nothing wrong with her. She told me she had been committed by her family and asked me to help her leave.

I agreed. By that stage I was allowed out during the day. I got a note signed by one of the doctors who liked me. One day I gave the nun my coat and scarf and one of the notes and she walked out. I never saw her again. A few weeks later I got a letter from her thanking me for my help. There were 10 crisp pound notes folded up in the letter.

A lot of the patients were alcoholics, very nice people who were the same as everyone else except they had a weakness for drink. One woman with whom I became friendly died as a result of her drinking and it greatly upset me. The upset was further exacerbated when a young man who was suffering from schizophrenia burned himself to death and two doctors also died. For a long time there was a terrible stench of death in the air and I became quite fearful of getting close to anyone in case they too would die. Although I was 17 I think I was emotionally very much younger.

I developed a keen interest in becoming a nurse and asked Ivor Browne to help me. A male nurse, John O'Reilly, a really decent man, also recommended me and with their help I became an auxiliary or cadet. I loved my job and began to receive wages which I saved in the post office. I wanted to train to be a geriatric nurse and worked mostly with old people, some of whom were senile, in the medical wing of the hospital. Others had simply been left there because their families couldn't, or wouldn't, care for them. I had my own room in the hospital and was free to go and come as I wished. One night in August 1967 one of the other auxiliaries suggested going to a charity concert in Marino. It was one of the very rare occasions I went out at night. Even for a sheltered girl like me the concert was not very exciting.

And then I set eyes on Father Michael Cleary for the first time. He was a local curate and very popular. He walked up on the stage and began cracking jokes. He was the life and soul of the party. He was so tall that you could see him from any part of the hall even if he wasn't on the stage. He had a receding hairline of wispy hair and hadn't yet grown his famous bushy beard. I was instantly taken by the big smile he had and the way he appeared full of the joys of life. He exuded a warmth which made people feel comfortable with him. He began singing the song *Living Doll*. Michael would never have been a contender for the Eurovision Song Contest but I liked his singing all the same. I watched him with interest from the side of the hall. I had never seen a priest so full of life and fun before. Any of them I had met up to then were dour and dull. I had a deep reverence for priests coming as I did from a strict Catholic ethos. The only men I trusted were priests because they were good men of God.

I was very impressed with Michael Cleary and thought that I would like him to hear my confession. I didn't look at him in a physical way, I felt no physical attraction for any man, especially a priest. I never thought about sex or a relationship at any time. I believed that up to that moment I had never made a proper confession. I saw the singing priest on stage as a very genuine man and the kind of person I could talk to.

After the show my friend introduced me to Michael. I don't think he remembered her but, as I would learn, he was very good at bluffing his way out of situations like that. I had to almost strain my neck to look up at him as he towered over me with that warm smile across his face. He made me feel like I was the only person in the world at that moment. No one had ever done that to me before. He seemed genuinely glad to have met me. He shook hands again and told me that if I was ever around Marino to pop in for 'a cup of tea and a chat'.

A few days later I wrote him a letter asking if he would hear my confession. I had been too shy to ask at the concert and I was very nervous. A day later I got a note from Michael telling me to call around on the following Saturday. I called to his parochial house just off Griffith Avenue beside the church of St Vincent de Paul where he was attached as a curate. It was a semi-detached house with a bay window in the front and a weeping willow on either side of the driveway. Michael opened the door with a smile and welcomed me to his home.

He shook my hand and gave me a peck on the cheek at the same time. No man had ever done that to me before. I was a little taken aback. 'This is an open house, the more people who call the better, that's the way I like it,' he reassured me. He showed me into his study and sat down. It wasn't a particularly luxurious room but I felt immediately comfortable there. A big desk his mother had had made for his ordination fitted into the bay window. On the opposite wall were two large bookcases, a hunting table, two or three armchairs, a few footstools and a television. We sat opposite each other in two armchairs beside the open fireplace with a roaring coal fire which gave the room great warmth. Tea was prepared and we talked about general things, but mostly my work in the hospital.

During the next two hours I found myself spilling out my heart to this priest I hardly knew. He was warm and understanding. His facial expressions said more than words. He was horrified that so much had happened in my short life and after all that my world was confined to inside the grounds of a psychiatric hospital, and that I had no friends or anywhere to go after work. At one stage when I was sobbing my heart out he leaned forward and put his hand on mine. 'God bless you, you poor child, no one should have to go through what you've been through,' he said. It was the first time a person paid so much attention to what I had to say. He was interested in me as an individual. All my life I had believed myself a worthless person with no particular purpose.

When it was time to leave I took the tea tray to the kitchen and washed up. It was a simple kitchen but I remember thinking to myself that it could be a little nicer. The conversation became lighter and a few times in between the phone interrupted the flow. His laughter from the hall brought a smile to my face. As I was leaving Michael opened the door for me and stroked my cheek with his finger. Then he said the nicest words I had ever heard. 'I am out quite often, all over the place in fact, but I want you to come by anytime you feel

like it . . . I want you to treat this house as if it was your own.'
I could not believe my ears and thought that he wasn't being
serious. But the look in his face and the warmth in his voice
and smile told me he was being sincere. Afterwards I worried
if he had been feeling sorry for me when he heard my
confession. I remember skipping lightheartedly to the bus stop
smiling to myself like a Cheshire cat. I was happier than I had
been in a long time.

From that moment on I went to Michael's house every
chance I could get. When I was off duty I would get ready to
go and visit and I would look at the others with an attitude
that said 'That shook you, I have some place to go where I am
welcome and wanted'. When I stood at the number 24 bus stop
on Abbey Street I was always happy and felt like I was going
home. Often when I arrived Michael would be going out. He
would give me a friendly kiss on the cheek as always and tell
me to help myself. 'Do anything you want,' he would say with
a generous smile. I would go into the kitchen and make myself
some tea and then go and watch whatever I liked on TV. No
one, except those who lived a similar institutionalised life, will
understand how incredible it is to be able to be able to do such
simple things in a normal house. Life was almost as perfect as
it could have been. The house was always buzzing with people
coming and going. Michael was working at the time with a
support group for unmarried mothers called Ally. Girls would
stay in the spare room of the house until it was time for them
to have their babies. In those days it was considered a scandal
for a girl to have a baby out of wedlock. In the vast majority of
cases they gave them up for adoption. For a lot of them
Michael was their only refuge.

We would have long talks and Michael would listen to my
problems. Then he used to take me around the country to
concerts and charity functions where he was a guest celebrity.
I would bring a friend along for the fun. It was such an exciting
time. Sometimes I had to pinch myself when I wondered how
I had become friends with such a great, generous man. I didn't

feel worthy. Here was the little match girl from the orphanage, being driven around in style by this wonderfully charismatic priest who, despite his hectic life, had time to befriend a wretch like me. Over the next six weeks I stayed in the house the odd night and slept in the spare room.

And then one evening it happened out of the blue. He held and kissed me passionately at the door. Nothing like that had ever happened to me before. Then I found myself sitting beside him exchanging marriage vows. I was confused, scared and elated all at once. Everything had happened so quickly I was overwhelmed by it all. I was in love with a man whom I felt loved me. From what Michael had told me I was convinced that I was now married but it had to be a secret because my husband was a priest. But we still had to consummate our unique relationship before it would be recognised in the eyes of God.

After that evening I just lived to be with Michael every available moment. But I was extremely nervous about our next meeting which took place a few days later. It was in the afternoon when I called. Michael opened the door. As usual he was smiling. He was wearing his stock and collar under a cardigan. When he shut the door he lifted me off the ground and kissed me on the lips. This kiss was different to the first one. It was even more urgent and he seemed to shake with excitement. I felt scared of what was about to happen although I knew he would do no harm to me.

He took me by the hand and led me up the stairs which led past the spare room and into his bedroom. He closed the curtains as I looked around me. He hardly spoke as he checked one more time if there was anyone coming towards the house. The sheets were starched white with a dusty pink candlewick bedspread. The bed was an old-fashioned design somewhere between a double and single in size. There was a huge wardrobe, a tallboy and a dressing table. Next to the bed was a side table with a lamp. He began kissing me again and gently lowered me onto his bed. We did not undress, I was too shy.

He began touching me and encouraged me to touch him. I felt very uncomfortable with this but he reassured me that I would get used to it. Michael had become my teacher in the most intimate lesson in life.

He loosened his trousers and removed my under garments. He attempted penetration but not too hard because it was so painful for me. As a lover Michael was always gentle and considerate. And he appeared experienced, like he had done this before. He gave up with little success. Then he encouraged me to help give him relief because he had become so aroused. I hated it. I felt our relationship would not be complete until we had successfully made love. I loved Michael and I wanted to be able to make love with him. I was glad when it was over. But I had failed to satisfy Michael and consummate our love. 'What is wrong with me?' I kept asking myself. He reassured me: 'Don't worry about this, it's because you are a virgin and tight, it will take time and when it does eventually happen it will never hurt again.'

As the weeks went by we continued in our efforts to consummate our relationship. Michael seemed determined that we would succeed. I couldn't help feeling a sense of inadequacy. I gradually began to feel less inhibited in his company and took off more of my clothes. I had grown up with no knowledge of sex. All that I knew was modesty and during the years we were together I did not like him seeing me naked before we got into bed. Then after about three months it finally happened – we managed to succeed in making love. I didn't enjoy it much because it hurt terribly. But Michael kissed me and said that it would never be painful again. Afterwards I began to cry because I started bleeding. I had no idea what happened when you finally lost your virginity. I was terribly embarrassed but Michael comforted me as he lay down beside me. He seemed so happy and fulfilled that our relationship had finally been consummated.

He got up and told me to go and have a wash in the bathroom. Then he removed the stained sheets and got dressed himself. We sat downstairs for a while and had tea. I was still embarrassed and confused about what was going on. Michael put his hand on my leg and said I was fine. Later he drove me back to St Brendan's in his Corsair car. I asked him: 'Does this mean that we are finally married?' 'Of course it does. . . that's what makes a marriage but we must keep this a secret, that is very important,' he replied. He held my hand as he drove. When he dropped me off he repeated the need for keeping our special relationship a secret. He said goodbye and drove off. I was happy in a sense but there was an immediate sense of sadness that I had to suppress the joy I felt in my heart. I had given him my virginity, which for me was like giving him my soul and I loved him desperately.

In the years after that I grew so used to Michael, just like any other wife. I considered the sexual side of our relationship a small price to pay for the feeling of being loved for the first time in my life. Being wanted and needed made me feel like a very special person. I loved his smell, the smell of his pillow and sheets and his clothes. I wanted to do everything for him and just be by his side. In hindsight I could not have loved him more but he could have loved me a lot more. He had a high sex drive and made love to me quite a lot.

But I was third on his list of priorities, the priesthood came first, then his performing and I was last. I had severe difficulty carrying the burden of our secret. After all I had experienced in my life which I didn't want to share with anyone, I found myself forced to keep secret the most special thing to ever happen to me. I couldn't understand why we had to live apart when we had shared secret vows. I didn't think there was anything wrong with our relationship although I knew that it would be construed as a scandal. As far as I was concerned it was God who had brought us together.

At the same time my efforts to become a trainee nurse had been seriously hampered by some members of the staff who objected to my appointment on the grounds that I had also been a patient. I was dreadfully upset when I was left with little option but to give up my ambition. I was completely disillusioned and scared. The route I had mapped out for myself in life was suddenly put off limits to me. When I told Michael he fobbed me off by saying that things would work out and I was so young I had my whole life in front of me. At that time the Eastern Health Board had opened a hostel or halfway house for former patients. From there I did courses in shorthand and typing.

There was a mixture of people in the hostel, most of them though were alcoholics who were recovering. They were all very nice people with one thing in common, all of us were hurt people. Then around November 1968 we were told that there was to be two flag days for the Rehabilitation Institute which was helping us find skills. We were told that everyone was expected to participate. From the first time it happened I had tremendous difficulty with my menstrual cycle. Every month I went through a terrible time for three or four days. On the flag day I was too ill to go and thought that I would not be missed.

I had decided to call Ivor Browne to see if he could recommend some medication to help me cope. Before I called him a social worker arrived at the hostel and said Ivor wanted to see a few of us. I was glad because I said I wanted to see him anyway. By this stage Ivor knew of my relationship with Michael but he was very much against it. He advised me to get out and make a new start in my life. He was very annoyed that he had put so much work into helping me get my act together and now I was involved in a dangerous liaison. I tried to reassure him that everything was fine and I would get out. In my mind I knew that what he was saying was true but I didn't want to acknowledge that.

In St Brendan's I waited outside Ivor's office until it was my turn to meet him. I was curious to know what he wanted to see me about. When I went in Ivor was standing beside his desk. He was obviously angry about something. 'After what I have heard I am left with no alternative but to lock you up, Phyl,' he told me in a stern voice. I was completely gobsmacked by his words. But I had no idea what it was that I was supposed to have done and to this day I still don't know. Ivor now accepts that he had been given a damning report about my activities and had acted on that information. He believes that he may have been mistaken that day. The door to Ivor's secretary's office was open and a large, familiar nurse was standing there waiting to take me away. I looked back at Ivor with tears streaming down my face and said: 'No one is going to take me anywhere.' At that Ivor asked if I would go with him. I agreed.

He opened the door to his office and I ran out past him. I ran and ran. I had had enough of hospital and this time I was going to stay free. I ran down the road which leads from the hospital and hid in a laneway, glued myself to the wall. I was terrified. I saw Ivor's car driving up and down and also the social worker's car. I didn't have time to think anymore about what I was supposed to have done.

I continued running. I moved from garden to garden along North Circular Road to avoid detection. In the distance I saw one of the nurses standing by his car looking around for a glimpse of me. I crouched down in a garden but worried that the house owner would spot me and send me packing. I saw a bus and jumped out on to the road and made for it. I thought the nurse saw me and as soon as the bus stopped I darted into a side street in case he had followed me. I made it to my friend Phyl's house, to seek help, but she wasn't home. I would have given anything to rest but I kept on running. Eventually I went around to Michael's house but he wasn't home either but a friend of his told me he was having a retreat in Cabra at 8 p.m. I walked to the church where Michael was due to have the retreat. I was completely exhausted and starving because I hadn't eaten all day. On the way I stopped off in a café and bought a cup of Bovril with the few bob I had on me.

I went to the sacristy at 7.30 p.m. and met Michael briefly. There were a lot of people around and neither of us could say much. I told him excitedly about what had happened. He smiled and put his hand on my shoulder. 'Go back to my house, here is the key, and wait until I get home and we'll talk about it,' he replied in a comforting voice. He gave me money for the bus fares back to Marino. I got two buses and felt a little calmer now that Michael was helping me. It was dark when I got to the house. Michael came in about 9.30 p.m. We kissed for a few moments and then he suggested that I go up to bed and get a good night's sleep. I needed to rest so badly and I was glad to co-operate. I washed myself in the bathroom and was going into the spare bedroom when I heard Michael letting someone in downstairs. I couldn't hear who it was. I lay down on the bed with my head in my hands when Michael knocked on the door.

I expected that he wanted to come to bed with me. I wanted his arms wrapped around me and to feel his body next to mine. I needed to be held. Then my heart sank. Standing behind him was one of the night matrons from St Brendan's. Michael had betrayed me and called Ivor Browne. He had helped set me up. The night matron was a very nice woman and I was at least glad that it had been her who was sent to fetch me. I looked at Michael with tears welling up in my eyes and asked, 'Why?' Then I looked at the statue of the Child of Prague on the mantelpiece and screamed out: 'Oh why, God?' I was given a few minutes to gather myself and leave with the matron. Outside they had an ambulance waiting for me. Michael's silence was deafening. Looking back on that incident I still do not know what it was that I was supposed to have done. Ivor Browne cannot remember either. Michael often apologised for what happened that day.

I was placed in a room with a single bed which resembled a cell. I was given a sleeping pill and the door was locked. I felt lonely and betrayed. The next morning my clothes were taken away. I went on a hunger strike for several days taking only tea or water. I eventually got my clothes back. During the weeks I was in the hospital I never saw either Ivor or Michael. The young doctor who was assigned to me was a very kind man.

He agreed with me that I wasn't insane and brought me picture calendars to put on the walls of my room to cheer it up a bit. I got friendly with one of the nurses and, when the young doctor was on duty, he gave me permission to stay over in the nurse's house where I babysat her children.

I did not know how to get myself out of this situation. I called Michael and berated him for betraying me. He was cold and distant but still agreed to help me. I was hurt and confused. On reflection I think he was glad to be rid of me. It was time for a new start in my life. I needed a change.

CHAPTER THREE

Our First Child

IN JANUARY 1969 I decided to make a break and try a new direction in my scattered life. Up to now it had been one of institutionalised hell between orphanages and psychiatric hospitals. The only good thing to happen to me had been Michael Cleary but after the episode in the previous November I felt that I couldn't trust him. I was alone, confused and sad. So, when I was released from St Brendan's I opted to go to London. I could only think of my survival and getting away so that I wouldn't have to go back to that hospital again. I hoped that I might find normality and stability somewhere else.

I told Michael that I was going because I had to get away. He didn't seem to mind my going. It was as if he just wanted rid of me at that stage. Michael wanted me sexually but he also probably considered me a threat to his safe world. I never saw myself as a threat to him or his career as a priest. He gave me the name of a man in London who would be happy to help me find a job and a place to stay. I was really scared. I was not in contact much with my family and I felt that I had no one to turn to. Michael and my friend Phyl took me to the boat in Dun Laoghaire. He just said goodbye, shook my hand and helped me with my luggage. I had three big suitcases with me. They were full of rubbish. I had never been anywhere in my life and just put everything I owned into those cases.

I will never forget that boat ride. I went into a state of shock. I didn't know really where I was going to go when I got to London. In those unenlightened days in Catholic Ireland London was seen as a godless place where all kinds of awful things happened to Irish girls. It didn't occur to me to wonder then why so many Irish people were taking the same boat. I had heard all these ridiculous stories about white slavery, about young women being taken off as sex slaves for wealthy Arabian sheikhs. I was petrified that I could be taken off the street and never seen again. I didn't talk to anyone for the whole trip. When people spoke to me it was like I was looking through them.

When I got to Holyhead three Scandinavian blokes who had been holidaying in Ireland helped me with my heavy cases. On the train ride to London I was petrified. I didn't have time to think of Michael. I was too scared of what would happen if I couldn't get work. There were two men from the west of Ireland in the same carriage. They were friendly and I sat near them. Like me, they were going to London for the first time. I knew I would be safer in the company of people from my own country. We arrived in London's Euston Station at five or six in the morning. It was a cold, damp, misty morning. The darkened streets were quiet and the street lights cast eerie shadows on the empty pavements. The three of us went to an Irish Centre. It wasn't open for business until 9.30 a.m. We found a corner café and ordered tea and sandwiches. I can still get the taste of my first meal on English soil. The tea tasted like dish water and the sandwiches were like sawdust. We whiled away the few hours rambling around the area like lost sheep.

When the centre opened the contact person Michael had put me in touch with interviewed me about what kind of work I wanted to do. I couldn't do much except clean and keep a house. I had some experience of nursing but had experienced difficulties getting a position as a trainee nurse back in Ireland.

I sat around till the afternoon when I was told that an interview had been arranged for me for a job as an au pair. I was given directions to a house in Ealing and left to find my own way. I waited in the pouring rain for half an hour before I got a cab. When I arrived at the house I was dripping wet. The lady of the house was Spanish and married to an Irish doctor. They were a really nice couple. The interview lasted a few minutes and then she showed me to my room. I was to start work immediately. I felt a great sense of relief and the anxiety which had gripped my body faded. I got dried and then met the children. They were lovely, two boys and a baby girl, Julian, Adrian and little Emma. I grew very close to them although whenever the woman of the house spoke in Spanish on the telephone, in my insecurity, I wondered if she was talking about me.

I rarely went out and on the few occasions I did, they were bad experiences. A girl I had met through the Irish Centre invited me over to her flat one Sunday afternoon. She lived in Dollis Hill. On trips like this I was always frightened. I knew it was stupid to feel that way but I couldn't help it. My friend gave me directions on which underground trains to take. I got totally mixed up. When I went to the tube station in Ealing I got on the first train that came without checking if it was the right one. I knew I had to change trains and I would get off at a station and go back and pay another fare. I didn't know that once I paid my fare from Ealing to Dollis Hill that was all I had to pay. It cost me a fortune. I was completely lost and in tears when I finally gave up and phoned her. I felt so stupid. My friend gave me more directions and met me in another tube station. I had left the house in Ealing at 11 a.m. When I finally met my friend it was 6 p.m.

Michael wrote a letter to me asking how I was. I couldn't tell if he was missing me or not. He signed it with the number '8' which was the number of letters in the words 'I love you'. It would remain our secret code for the rest of our lives together. He never phoned. Then one night I got the shock of my life when I saw him on television. He was in London for some show with Hughie Green. I was gutted. He was over here and hadn't bothered to call me. As the weeks went by I began to miss home and Michael, even though I was angry at him for not getting in touch. I quit my job in May and took the boat home. It was the beginning of a pattern which would occur many times during my life with Michael Cleary.

When I came back I stayed with my mother for a brief time in Ballymun. There had never been much of a loving relationship between us and I spent the shortest possible time in her company. I got a job in Roches Chemist on Grafton Street. I also got a bedsit on Castle Avenue in Clontarf. It was a tiny room, with a single bed, a sink and a cooker, but at least it was my little part of the world. It was a busy pharmacy and we were paid on a commission basis. I didn't really like the job much. I was still scared of the world and totally naïve. My colleagues in the chemist talked a lot about going out to pubs and dances and often asked me if I would go with them. But I was too scared. In hindsight I was an absolute prude and knew nothing about life. I did not approve of night-clubbing or of women drinking. In my mixed-up head I thought it was a sin for a woman to go into a public house while at the same time being secretly 'married' to a priest. My colleagues kept on asking me to go out on the town until it became too much. One Thursday a few of them said that I was going out that night and they would not take no for an answer. They saw how sheltered and innocent I was and were just being good natured to me. But I didn't see it that way. That evening I left the shop and never returned.

At the same time my relationship with Michael resumed on its haphazard route to an unknown destination. When I came home from London I rang him. He seemed glad to hear from me. I told him I was angry that he had not bothered to contact me when he was over for the television show. He explained that he had rushed to London at the last moment and didn't have time to call anyone. Michael always had a way of making convincing excuses and I believed him. I was in love with him and I needed to trust him. Michael could have told me he was God and I would have believed him.

Shortly after coming home I met him in the Crofton Hotel for coffee. I was excited about seeing him again. He had a big beaming smile on his face and made me feel special. He was rushing off somewhere and arranged for me to call to see him a few days later when he came back. I called by the house in the afternoon. Michael was in the house on his own. He opened the door the same as he had done so many times before. There was a twinkle in his eye, he was excited with anticipation of being with me again. His reaction made me excited too. I wanted to feel his arms around me again. We went up to his bedroom and closed the curtains. For the next few hours we made love. It was one of the occasions I can recall really enjoying sex with Michael. I was glowing inside. Feeling his flesh against mine, the taste of his lips, his arms held tightly around me, his hands exploring my body, I shivered in ecstasy. We were a husband and wife again in the eyes of God. I forgave him as our bodies joined together. I felt loved.

From the time I first met Michael he brought me around the country to his concerts. I got to see the country on those trips and I really enjoyed myself. Michael always ensured that I brought a friend. We never travelled to concerts on our own in case it would make people suspicious. Michael never let his guard down. The venues were parish halls, ballrooms and marquees which were particulary popular during summertime in the 1960s and early '70s. When he was on stage telling jokes and singing a few songs Michael would joke that: 'I've a couple of lovely Dublin girls with me tonight looking for fellahs.' I would be mortified, especially when blokes would come looking for the Dublin girls.

Now and again we would stay in a local hotel or guest house if the concert was very far away. One night we stayed in a little seaside village, called Owenahincha, about two hours drive south-west of Cork city. My sister Tricia came with us.

During the concert Michael made the remark that we were looking for two Corkmen. I was furious with him. This guy followed me around for the rest of the evening. He was the ugliest person I ever encountered. He looked like the character Fagin from Oliver Twist only without the beard. His friend wasn't much better and he began pursuing Trish. After the concert I decided to go back to the room because this guy was really annoying me. Trish was somewhere else and Michael was still having the crack with the local people. The Fagin lookalike followed me. When I got near my room he grabbed me and pushed me against the wall. I kicked him hard on the shin and he let me go. I ran to my room and locked the door. Michael laughed when I told him what happened but I warned him never to say that on stage again.

In July we went to a concert in County Wexford. Phyl, my friend came with us. Michael loved taking the scenic routes. It sometimes drove me mad. I thought they were enjoyable but not for three or four hours through Wicklow and Wexford. Michael would normally go on stage late and the concert wouldn't finish until midnight or 1 a.m. By the time I got home I would be exhausted. On this particular night we arrived back in Dublin around 2 a.m. We dropped Phyl off at her house and then Michael brought me back to Marino. There was no one staying in the house and the coast was clear. I was tired but Michael wanted to make love. I could never say no to him. We went to his room and made love under his candlewick bedspread. When it was over we fell asleep in each other's arms. It was one of the rare occasions when we actually spent a night together. I remember wanting that night to last forever because I knew when the morning came the façade would go up again. Things would go on as if nothing had happened. I felt so confused. I would think to myself: 'Here I am lying in the arms of the man I am married to in the eyes of God but I can't stay like this in case someone finds out.' I hated having to return alone to my cold little bedsit.

About a week later I was in a café in town having a coffee

when, like a bolt out of the blue, the thought entered my mind, 'I'm pregnant!'. It was just a feeling which came over me. But I was in for another shock. In my innocence I had never connected sex with pregnancy. In today's society it may seem unbelievable but I thought that sex was something you did when you were married and that God blessed the marriage by sending children. I thought that Michael's withdrawal at the end of our love-making was normal. In fact withdrawal was the only form of contraception we ever practised. At this stage I thought that God had alerted me to the fact that he had sent me a child. Later a smiling friend enlightened me. I felt like I had been conned.

Michael went pale when I told him in the front room of the house that I thought I was pregnant. His attitude towards me suddenly transformed. The expression of shock and disbelief on his face upset me and I began to cry. I couldn't understand his reaction, surely this was part of being married? He looked panicked: 'How do you know? Have you missed a period?' I was stunned that he knew things like that about a woman's body and told him that I just had a feeling I was pregnant. 'Let's wait and see if you are only imagining things. There is no point in panicking until you have definitely missed your cycle,' he assured me. I left the house feeling shattered. I felt that I had done something terribly wrong. I was learning the facts of life the hard way.

Over the next two weeks I began feeling very sick. When I missed my cycle I called Michael and told him. He grew cold and distant towards me. He was in a state of shock. Michael arranged for me to travel to see a doctor in Waterford for a pregnancy test. He didn't want me to tell anyone, especially Ivor Browne. He knew that Ivor disapproved of our relationship and would be concerned about the situation. So he put me on a train to Waterford. When I got there I discovered that the doctor I was going to see had gone to Dublin. When I came back Michael sent me to a gynaecologist in Fitzwilliam Square.

I was confirmed pregnant a few days later. The baby, our baby, was due in March. Michael's attitude to what was happening brought back that awful feeling of isolation and loneliness which has shadowed me all my life. He suggested that I go back to London to get out of sight. Michael sent me to a friend of his, a man called Casey (no relation of Eamonn Casey) who would help me get fixed up in a job. He was a very nice man. To him I was just another poor wretch of a girl who had got into trouble and was being helped out by Michael. After all he was well known for providing refuge and assistance to young, unmarried mothers.

The first job I got was in a small hotel in central London. I was shown to a hostel for the staff where I was to share a room. The room was awful, the floor was bare and there was a big ugly wardrobe which I had to share with a stranger. The next morning I began working as a chambermaid. Everything went fine until lunch time. I went into the staff canteen to eat. The place was so filthy I was nauseated and disgusted. The floor was covered with scraps of food. The food looked awful and I couldn't force myself to eat it. I ran to throw up in the toilet. I packed my bags and went back to Michael's friend again. He got me another job the same day, this time as a chambermaid in the more upmarket Regent's Palace Hotel in Piccadilly. The manager was very nice to me and said I was more housekeeper material than chambermaid. Trainee housekeeper was the job I preferred and I was blessed to get it. Generally, applicants for the job had to be 24 and I was still only 19 years old.

The staff were looked after superbly. I had a beautful room to myself. It was tastefully decorated in royal blue, white and tangerine. There was a maid service and outside my room a cooler with ice-cold milk, the only thing cool in London that year. It was a very hot, humid summer. The food in the staff canteen was almost better than that being served to the guests. The head housekeeper referred to us as 'administrators'. There was a value placed on staff and it was a happy working environment. Everyone made me feel welcome and secure. It was the first time that had ever happened to me. But all the time I was fearful that someone would discover I was pregnant. Michael rang once or twice to see how I was. He seemed glad that I was happy with my work. In my naïvete I thought that he was happy for me, but upon reflection it was more like he was glad his mistake was out of sight and out of mind.

As the weeks went by I suffered more from nausea and vomiting. I also had stomach ulcers. I was too afraid to attend a doctor or talk to anyone about it. Then one day I fainted in the bathroom. I decided that I would have to leave because I couldn't work any longer. I told the head housekeeper but she tried to persuade me to stay. Under different circumstances I would have stayed in that job and made a career for myself. For the second time in a year I was on my way back to Dublin, Michael. . . and an uncertain future.

When I arrived back the streets were littered with the golden colours of autumn leaves. At first Michael arranged for me to stay at the home of a friend of his until there was space in his house, which was still being used as a refuge for unmarried mothers. After a few weeks I moved into Michael's house. I slept on a fold-up bed in a small room inside the front door which Michael used for interviewing people. I blended in well because there were two other girls in the house at the time. They were in the spare room which had two single beds. One day I went to confession in a church in town. I was feeling lonely, depressed and guilty. I told the priest that I was pregnant with the child of a priest. I wanted to confess. I couldn't have expected the response from the priest on the other side of the grille. He began ranting at me that he didn't believe me. He called me a whore and an evil bitch and ordered me out of the church. I was devastated and cried my heart out.

The next few months were among some of the loneliest of my life. When the other girls were visited by family or friends I would have to make myself scarce. I only had a few friends in the world and I wasn't very close to my family. I couldn't face the questions about the identity of the father of my child so it was best to keep contact with the outside world to a minimum. Michael's sister Marita was one of those who was particularly nice to me. She often helped the unmarried mothers. But there was no way he had told her about our situation and she didn't suspect anything. Michael had grown distant although on a few odd occasions, when the house was empty, he made love to me in his room.

He suggested that when I had the baby the best thing would be to put it up for adoption. He said that I was too young to rear a child. I agreed with Michael. From the time I met him he had total control over me. I didn't know any difference because I had never been told anything about life. I couldn't question what was happening because I didn't know what should be happening. And I was terrified that if I did raise my voice or attract attention our secret would be revealed and both of us condemned by a world which didn't want to understand our love. I am not angry towards Michael for how he was. In a lot of ways he was as innocent as I was, even if he was 17 years older. He must have been so scared and panicked.

On the morning of Friday, 20 March 1970, I went into labour. It was a fresh, crisp day. I started getting cramps as soon as I awoke. I wasn't quite sure at the time what they were. When I told Michael, he said: 'Oh God, you are probably starting labour.' There was another priest in the house visiting Michael and as my pains got worse he innocently remarked: 'Good God, I would never do anything like that to a woman.' I looked at Michael and tried to smile. Neither of us said anything. Around 11.30 a.m. Michael drove me to the nursing home where I had been booked in. He looked nervous, but not half as nervous as I was. He left me with the nurses and went off.

I paced up and down the room on my own for another couple of hours and then I was given medication to ease the pain. I was groggy when I was brought into the labour ward. I was in so much pain that I just wanted to scream 'cut me' to get it over with. The doctor kept telling me to hold the gas mask over my mouth and I said I couldn't because it was too heavy. My son was born at 3.25 p.m. that same afternoon. I didn't see him. When I asked the nurses where he was they said he was being cared for in the nursery. Although I had agreed to put him up for adoption I wanted to hold my baby. But this was the normal procedure in these situations. I was also too scared to open my mouth because I didn't want to give anything away.

On the following day Michael came to visit. He was glad to see that I was in good form. He assured me that the baby was all right and being looked after well. He said that I was doing the right thing by allowing the baby to find a good home with adoptive parents. He brought in a TV so that I could watch the Eurovision song contest. That night Dana won with 'All Kinds of Everything'. Everytime I hear that song I think of our first son. I finally got to see the baby for the first time on the following Tuesday. He had dark hair and blue eyes. He was beautiful. I only got to spend five to ten minutes with him. When I left the nursery my heart sank to my toes. I was in a daze. 'Is that really my baby?' and 'Did this really happen to me?' were the questions running through my head.

I registered the baby in the name Michael Ivor after Michael Cleary and Ivor Browne, the two men who had played major roles in my life up to that time. Then I named a doctor I knew as the father of the child and put myself down as a nurse because I felt the child would get a better home if his parents were seen to be qualified medical professionals. A week after the birth I saw my baby for the last time. Michael and my friend Phyl collected me with Michael Ivor and brought us to Marino. Michael christened his little son. It was a very solemn ceremony with no flashing cameras or cheerful smiles. There were just three of us around the baptism font. I can't recall much about how Michael reacted because I was so wrapped up in my own feelings. I was holding my beautiful little baby knowing that in a short time I would be giving him away. Michael would have had to be some kind of automaton not to have felt something for the son he too would never see again. Michael was always a caring, loving man and I can only believe that he was going through his own personal hell.

As soon as the baptism was over a friend of Michael's picked me up and drove us to the adoption home. It was a long, lonely journey. I cradled this little tot in my arms close to my heart. He was so peaceful and quiet, hardly stirring. I tried not to look at him but couldn't resist it. My mind was racing, ready to explode. Everyone around was saying that I was too young to have this child, that I was an unfit mother and the best place for him was somewhere else. But my maternal instincts told me they were wrong, that I must keep this baby. I felt powerless to protest; I had no control over what was happening.

In the adoption home I handed over Michael Ivor to a nun. It was such a symbolic gesture. It was like I was handing over my soul. I was numb. So many young Irish women did the same thing for so many years in an age when it was considered a stigma to have a child out of wedlock. That made my sin even worse . . . my baby was the product of a priest's forbidden love. Nowadays people whinge and moan about the numbers of unmarried mothers in Ireland. That is because the vast majority of girls will not be told what to do with their babies any longer and are instead opting to rear them themselves. Everytime I see a young mother like that I feel like going up and saying, 'Well done girl – I wish to Christ when I was your age I had the same courage.'

At first he had led me to believe that the baby would be placed with a family for six months to allow me to arrive at my final decision on whether I wanted to go ahead with the adoption. Ever since that heart-wrenching moment when I handed over my baby I wanted him back. Three weeks later I phoned the home where he was. I asked if I could go to see him. The woman who answered the phone took my head off when I told her what I wanted. 'You selfish little bitch, that baby has gone to a very good home and you should be very grateful,' the cruel voice replied down the line. I put down the phone. I was in tears and furious with Michael. 'Why didn't you explain this to me properly instead of some stranger telling me I'm a selfish bitch, that somebody else has my baby?' I demanded to know. He argued with me that the baby was better off with a family, that I was too immature to rear a child. I began to believe that he was right. All my life I had no confidence in myself, self-esteem was a luxury I could not afford. I was being a failure as a person, what would I be like as a mother?

Life continued to amble along and although I was angry and hurt by what had happened I still loved Michael. I never got much of an opportunity to discuss it with him because there was so much going on in the house. We slept together from time-to-time. I stayed on in the house for a while because it was normal for mothers to stay for a while afterwards to get back their strength before returning home. In May I got a job in an old folk's home as a nurse's aid. It was my way of taking my mind off Michael Ivor. I loved the work and spent a lot of my time there. I slept there a lot in the nurses' quarters and divided the rest of the time in Michael's house.

In August I decided that I was not going to go ahead with the adoption. I again called the adoption agency and said I had changed my mind, that I wanted my baby back. Again I was berated for being selfish and told: 'You can't do this to people – you can't take a child away from a family who have had it for nearly six months.' I cried bitter tears all that day until I fell asleep. Michael went into a rage when I told him I had second thoughts. Again he told me how immature I was. It was the same damn line all the time. It was like I was being brainwashed. I was angry with Michael and also with God.

When the notification came the following month that I had to sign the adoption papers, I refused. Michael again went into a rage at me. Then he threatened that if I continued refusing to sign he would take the child away from me, leave the priesthood and go away. I would never see either him or the baby again. I was shattered by what he said. I didn't realise that he was pressurising me into it – that he just wanted rid of the responsibility and the danger of being exposed. There was no way he was going to leave the Church. I was not getting any support from anyone.

When he cooled down a bit Michael tried to reassure me. He said that I shouldn't worry about the adoption because the child had gone to a 'fabulous family' although he said he didn't know who they were. I have often wondered since Michael's death if he knew the family who adopted his first son and whether he had the luxury of watching him growing up from a distance. Then he reassured me that 'there will be more children down the road'. Those words gave me a new optimism and helped me get over the despair which was in my heart. I felt that Michael loved me and did want to have a child with me some day.

I will never forget the morning he brought me to sign away my child. It was one of the saddest days of my life as I walked into that cold, dingy little solicitor's office on the Quays. It was all so impersonal and took only a few minutes with hardly a word from anyone. It was like I was signing a form to sell a car. I felt so helpless. I had signed away control over my own life. I cried in the car on the way back to Marino. Michael didn't say a word. I will never know what was going on in his head.

In the days after that I tried to suppress the pain I felt. There was nothing I could do any more so I had to accept the situation and get on with life. I still clung to what Michael told me about the prospect of having more children. In the months which followed we went through a sort of tunnel and when we got to the other side our relationship continued. We got back to normal. Although our sexual relationship had never really stopped, when so-called normality was restored it became more regular. One afternoon in early 1971 I had to go back to the house in Marino to collect something before going back on duty at the nursing home. When I got to the house I could see Michael's car parked at the side of the house. I hoped there was no one else in the house and maybe we could have an hour or so alone together. When I went inside I couldn't see him. As I went upstairs I heard whispering and a woman giggling. It was coming from Michael's room. When I opened the door I was stunned by what I saw.

He was in bed with a woman, someone I knew personally. She had been one of the unmarried mothers he had counselled in the past. She was quite attractive but older than me, in her late 20s. Like me, she too had given up her baby for adoption. I could see they were both naked under the bedspread. She was on top of him. He was lying on his back; his eyes rolling around in his head. He groaned a little. Michael looked at me with an expression of suprise on his face. I ran out of the door before anything could be said, down the stairs and left, slamming the front door behind me. I was devastated that the man who had shared marriage vows with me could make love to another woman and in the same bed where I had given myself to him for the first time. The bed where he had ended my virginity. The same bed where Michael Ivor, our little adopted baby, had been conceived. As I raced back to work so many thoughts crowded my mind. I was disgusted and asked myself how many more women there were. I knew deep down that I was not Michael's first sexual encounter but thought that he was faithful only to me, especially after I had been through so much. Then I wondered if he had fathered other children. Was I just another one of his conquests?

I stayed in the nursing home that night and finally went back to Marino the following afternoon. Michael was on his own in the house. He looked at me sheepishly as I walked through the door. I hardly spoke to him. I was almost afraid to confront the issue because he had this way of getting around me. All through his life Michael had a way of explaining things to make them seem normal. He said that going to bed with the other woman was a one-off thing which just happened. It was 'one of those things' he told me. And, of course, as in most situations like this, it was the woman's fault, she had seduced him. At the time, however, I swallowed it hook, line and sinker and it was never mentioned again. Normality, or such that it was in our world, returned.

Michael was very charming and considerate after that and it wasn't long before I was back in his bed again. A few weeks later he threw a suprise 21st birthday party for me on 28 February. He had invited about a dozen people and I was totally taken aback. I was flabbergasted that I got a party to begin with and I really enjoyed myself. Michael gave me a beautiful charm bracelet and a key.

In March I gave up my job in the old folk's nursing home. At the same time Michael's official housekeeper went away to Canada and I got the job. I was no longer a charity case and I didn't have to worry about my motives for living under the same roof with him. I never forgot about Michael Ivor and missed him terribly. Michael never mentioned him after that. Perhaps he found it too painful, or maybe he was just relieved that he had got off the hook. It is something I will never know. My anger subsided. My love for Michael was much stronger than that and we both needed each other. Following the adoption I felt that he loved me more, or perhaps he began to love me. For the next two years life was relatively happy and we grew closer to each other.

CHAPTER FOUR

Back Together

IN MAY 1973 Michael got a phone call which would cause the first of a number of major changes in our secret life. He was to be moved to a new parish in Ballyfermot, across on the south-west side of Dublin. It was one of the relatively new, sprawling suburban developments built by the Corporation with a burgeoning population of 100,000. It was demanding work for a priest to look after the myriad needs of a flock so large. It was one of the largest parishes in terms of population in Ireland with one church, Our Lady of the Assumption, and eight to ten curates. (Since then it has been broken into two parishes with two churches.) They were faced with a mammoth challenge to ameliorate a new generation of people who were disillusioned by unemployment and lack of opportunities. There was also the emergence of disenchantment with the Church. Michael was the ideal man for the job. He was charismatic and appealed to young people.

He liked the idea of such a major new challenge in his promising career and I was glad for him, too. But by now I was beginning to think that maybe it was time for me to move away and start a new life for myself. In the past few years, while they were happy, nothing between Michael and myself had been sorted out. We just tended to go with the flow and the future was never discussed much. We were both probably too scared to even contemplate what fate had in store for us. We were making the most of the present.

I went with him to view his new accommodation in the presbytery which was near the church on Kylemore Road. It was a big, old house, typical of many presbyteries around the country. Inside it was a bit like a convent. It accommodated four priests. Three of them had their own bedroom and sitting-room and they shared the same kitchen. Everyone in the house shared the same bathroom. Because Michael was the senior curate he had his own sitting-room, bedroom and kitchen. The housekeeper's quarters were separated from the main house although as far as I recall there was no live-in housekeeper at the time. People used to come in to do the cooking and cleaning for the priests.

At first Michael assumed that I would move in and we would go on living as before. But I was already having enough difficulty living what I saw as a hypocritical lie. Living with him was one thing, but doing so while sharing a house with three other priests was too much to contemplate. I had wanted Michael to leave the priesthood and for us to live together properly as man and wife. It was something which was a source of much turmoil and upset in our lives together. On a number of occasions Ivor Browne tried to help us sort the situation out because he felt it could be destructive for both of us, but especially me.

Both he and Michael often met to discuss where it was going, but nothing changed. Michael wanted it both ways and had no problem living a double life. Ivor advised Michael that if he wanted to continue the relationship then he should leave the Church. He admonished me that if Michael did not leave, then I should make a new life for myself. In fact, Ivor was the one person who knew most about the intricacies of our secret lives and went out of his way to help us both. On one occasion Ivor arranged for us both to meet with Michael's old friend, Bishop Eamonn Casey. Ivor and Casey had met on a number of occasions in the Royal Dublin Hotel on O'Connell Street and Eamonn agreed to meet us.

We travelled down the country and stayed as his guests in his magnificent house in Kerry. Eamonn was a bubbly, cheerful character who liked to enjoy life. As far as I recall there was no discussion between the three of us about the relationship at all. Michael and Eamonn went off for their own private chats but I have no idea what was discussed. Following that weekend, nothing changed in our lives. We visited Eamonn together on a few more occasions for weekends away. He was the first cleric to know our secret and that was important to Michael. Ironically, less than twenty years later, it was Eamonn Casey who indirectly caused the greatest upheaval in our relationship, when Eamonn's affair with Annie Murphy became public. He had never told Michael his secret.

In any event I decided that now was the right time for a change in my life. It was a tormenting decision but I had to give it a try. We were in bed together in Marino when I told him of my decision to leave. He didn't want me to go and said that he was already working on getting a house of his own because he was the senior curate in the parish. But I had made my mind up and he accepted it. 'I don't want to lose you but I have no right to demand that you stay and live somewhere that your are uncomfortable,' he sighed. I planned to go to Boston to relatives and then on to Florida. I was sad at the thought of leaving the man I so loved but there was also a degree of excitement and apprehension of what lay ahead of me. Compared to my first trip to London I was now an older, more worldly-wise woman of 23 and no longer terrified of going away. I carefully packed Michael's belongings in big tea chests for the move.

The night before I was due to leave we made love like it was for the last time. It was beautiful but sad. Neither of us wanted to part but we both knew there was little alternative. He drove me to the airport. On the way there he held my hand. He kept checking I had everything I needed, tickets, money, he was a bit like a big brother fussing over me. When we got to the airport he walked me to the departure hall. When he was in public he kept up his guard as the priest. He shook hands and said goodbye. He shook my hand so tightly it was like he didn't want me to go. I could see the sadness in his face. I fought back the tears which were welling up in my eyes and there was a lump in my throat. At that instant both of us wanted to embrace but couldn't. He was the priest: I was the house-keeper. We looked into each other's eyes for a few moments until we were interrupted by the announcement that it was the check-in time for the flight.

I stayed for a month or so in Boston with family and then went to Florida to my friend Phyl. I took small, part-time jobs because I was in the country on a visitor's visa although I hoped to get a green card and more permanent work. Michael wrote and phoned me regularly. The loneliness in his voice cut deep into my heart. I wished that our separation would help him find the courage to do the right thing. I was desperately lonely for him and couldn't look at another man even though I was often asked out on dates. On one occasion he asked me if I would consider coming home and I said that I couldn't when he was still in the same place. 'I couldn't be happy there, Michael,' I told him.

In August I decided to come home for a while. I hadn't been successful in getting a job and wanted to use the opportunity to see a friend who was home from Rome. But I mainly wanted to see Michael. A few days after I came back I went with my friend Mary to see him. We met for lunch in the West County Hotel in Chapelizod. I couldn't wait to see him I was so excited. We couldn't embrace each other because it was so public, but I could see that he couldn't wait to kiss me. He shook my hand and I could see that he was delighted that I was home again.

After lunch we left Mary off somewhere and I went back to the presbytery. When we got into his rooms we kissed and held each other for the longest time. 'I really missed you – I thought I would never see you again,' he said. When I looked around his rooms I got the shock of my life. The place was an absolute mess. Most of the boxes and tea chest I had packed for him were still lying in the same spot they were the day he moved in three months earlier. The kitchen was an absolute mess and didn't appear to have been cleaned for a very long time. It had a cooker, a small table and two chairs. Everything was filthy. In the sink there were piles of dirty dishes, some of which had mould on them. The fridge was worse. It had a few half empty milk bottles, one of which had a layer of green mould. There were a couple of eggs and some butter.

I said: 'My God, Michael, it looks like you haven't done much cleaning or got anyone in either to do it for you, why?' 'It's because there is only one woman who can look after me and that is you,' he replied. Then he asked me to stay but I said I couldn't, I had to make a new life for myself. There were tears in his eyes and he bent down on one knee and held my two hands in his, like he was proposing marriage. 'I wish you would stay but if you really cannot, at least help me get set up here . . . you are the only one who knows how to sort me out,' he implored me.

So I went to work straightaway. It was around 5 p.m. and Michael had to go out on parish business. I didn't know where to start in that kitchen it was in such a dreadful state. For over twelve hours I washed and scrubbed and scraped the dirt on the floor, the tops and the delph. Then I tried to put some order into his living-room. He came back around 5 a.m. after being out playing poker after his duties. No matter how preoccupied Michael ever was with the secret side of his life he always found time to play cards or follow the horses.

When he came in he couldn't believe his eyes at the transformation. I was sitting drinking tea and feeling very tired. He lifted me up and kissed me. 'Now you know why I love you and need you with me,' he said. There was an old familiar twinkle in his eyes which I had known ever since those first tentative attempts to surrender my virginity. He was excited and I could see he wanted me. I couldn't wait to feel his body next to mine. We sneaked to his bedroom and I got another shock. The place was in a heap. Clothes were thrown around the place, there were more boxes which I had carefully packed and there was an overflowing ashtray. I reckoned that he had given up using it when it filled up because there was cigarette ash and butts everywhere.

Then I saw the bed was a right mess, too. There was one sheet on it which was folded so that it could be used under and over. The blankets were thrown back in a pile. 'I don't believe this Michael . . . where are all your friends to help you fix this, place up?' I exclaimed. Michael looked into my eyes and held me close. 'I was waiting for you and have prayed every day that you would come home to me,' he said and then started kissing me passionately. I forgot about the state of the place and soon we were undressed and making love on that messed-up bed of his. It was the most natural progression. Later that same morning Michael had to get up and go to Mass, he was full of the joys of spring. He kissed me and warned me to be careful the other priests didn't see me. That was the poker player coming out. He often took risks like that when we were together even though he lived in terror that our relationship would be discovered. I had to stay in his messed-up room without making a sound until I knew the coast was clear and I could leave. I couldn't even go to the bathroom because all four of them in the house shared it between them.

Over the next two weeks or so I worked hard getting Michael set up in his new home. When the fortnight was up we had settled back into the old familiar regime. I was his housekeeper and his lover again. It was like fate had meant that we just kept falling back into each other's lives again. Throughout the years, Michael always said that it was the will of God that we were together and I still believe that. When it came to the time for me to leave I could see that Michael was anxious to hear if I would stay. When I told him he threw me up in the air and kissed me so hard it hurt my teeth. He was over the moon. After that I set up a room for myself and resumed working as a housekeeper.

From then on I began running Michael's life for him. He hadn't to worry about anything except his duties and other people's problems. I cooked his meals, cleaned his clothes and organised his appointments. I became really happy in Ballyfermot. There was a great atmosphere in the parish because all the priests worked as a team. They were all very nice men and there were plenty of laughs. In early 1974 we finally moved into a new house around the corner from the church. It was a detached three-bedroom house at 77 Colepark Drive.

Both of us were kept very busy there. The house was bustling with people coming to see Michael with some problem or other. He had a great big heart and loved people. After we moved we slept together practically all the time, unless someone was staying. In many ways we were like a normal couple when no one was around. The one thing which used to irritate me about sleeping with him was during the winter nights when he came home late from playing cards or a show and got into bed beside me with freezing cold feet. He would rub them on my legs to warm them up, waking me in the process.

But we had other problems with burglaries. The house was ransacked on several occasions during those years and was maliciously set on fire once while I was in it. It was as if our every move was watched. As soon as we both left the house, the burglars were in. The first burglary the thieves took all Michael's football trophies, my record player, records and a camera. At Mass the following Sunday, Michael made a plea from the altar for the return of his trophies – they were of no financial value but were sentimental value. Two days later, around 10 p.m., there was a knock on the door. I went out and found no one there. I stood there in the freezing cold wondering who had knocked. An eerie chill came over me and I felt someone watching me. Then I looked down and just to the side of the door was a large sack containing all Michael's trophies.

Michael was over the moon when he came home. The next time they struck they took nothing belonging to Michael but all my stuff. They even took my underwear. They also took a new sheepskin coat Michael had bought me. The police came and took statements and fingerprints but nothing ever came of it. Another time, when I had flu, I was supposed to go out for a meal with Michael and some friends. I didn't go because I felt so rotten. Earlier that day some teenagers had been throwing stones at the glass-house in the back garden. Michael caught them and gave them a few wallops. Just before he went out to dinner we heard a loud noise somewhere around the house. We both investigated but found nothing. I kissed him goodnight and went to watch television.

During the programme I heard a loud gurgling sound which appeared to come from the central heating pipes which ran under the floor in the sitting-room. I decided to switch it off in case there was a problem. I went into the hall and opened the kitchen door to find it full of smoke. The place was on fire. I went into panic and didn't know what to do. I closed the door again and ran out of the house and over to the church. The garage at the back of the house was engulfed with flames. Just as I got to the church door there was a big explosion and the glass doors blew out across the path I had run along only seconds before. I banged on the sacristy door and screamed and cried, I was so terrified. The alarm was raised and the fire brigade were there minutes later and saved the house. The closed kitchen door prevented it from spreading. I was very shaken after that. The police caught the culprits who started the fire. Years later, I remember Michael receiving a letter from one of the ringleaders apologising for what they did. He forgave them.

By this time Michael was fast becoming a household name in Ireland. He was one of the main movers behind the hugely popular *All Priests' Show* which toured the country playing in parish halls and community centres to raise cash for charities. He was also a regular on TV shows like the *Late Late Show* and would later begin writing columns for various newspapers. He was seen as one of a new breed of high profile priests in Ireland. He was regarded as outspoken, progressive and liberal, but at the same time faithfully adhering to the teachings of the Church he loved.

Michael revelled in the adulation and respect he got. He deserved it but, at the same time, he was being placed on a pedestal by an adoring public which placed immense pressure on him. He felt compelled to live up to those superficial expectations and it added to his fears that our love would be exposed. At the same time he did not want to end the relationship but very much wanted to keep it going. He needed me as much as he needed his Church and his status. They were three very important things to Michael Cleary. But I tended to help keep his feet on the ground. I had no problem telling him what he was when I saw him getting a bit too high. He would laugh and say that I was the only person in the world who could keep his feet firmly attached to the planet. Through the years Michael always depended on my judgment of people who came into our home. There were times when I caught people out trying to exploit Michael's generosity and sent them packing.

In the summer of 1974 Michael went on holiday to his sisters who were living in Canada. Before he went he was worried about a lump on his Adam's apple. He was a chain smoker and I was afraid of cancer. During the holiday he spent some time in Las Vegas, which to him was paradise because he was a serious gambler. On 28 June he wrote me a letter from the Stardust Casino and Hotel where he was staying. In it he broke the news that his sister Kathleen's husband, John Keohane, a doctor, had diagnosed a malignant growth on his thyroid gland. The letter, which was on the hotel-headed paper, read:

Dear Phyllis,

How do you like my notepaper? I've had a fabulous time here, I've seen all the shows, met all kinds of stars and I'm a few dollars ahead!

I'm going back to Canada today and will leave for Ireland on 3 July, arriving morning of 4 July. I have a booking on Aer Lingus from New York but still may get on the Montreal-Dublin flight with Kay, Marita, etc., as it's easier to get home that way from Edmonton. If anybody's looking for me put them off for a few days as I'll need time to re-adjust. The temperature here is 108 degrees, it's almost impossible to go outdoors except in an air-conditioned car. I've had just about enough of heat and idleness and I'm looking forward very much to going home.

One piece of news that isn't great is that I will have to have an operation soon after I return. Remember I used to joke about my Adam's apple? Patricia used to worry about it. Well, John examined it and it's a growth which must come out. However, I don't believe it can be very serious. John says a day or two should do it so I'm not worrying. I suppose I shouldn't write news like that to you but I just felt like telling somebody.

There's a big fellow called Salvador here and he's coming to Ireland soon. He'll stay in 'Ballyer'. I told him you would look after him well – he's looking forward to that. He's an excitable sort of guy but I think you'll enjoy him. That's all the news for now, God Bless, Michael.

When I read the letter I was frantic with worry about him. But I was also angry that he hadn't had the operation while in Canada with his brother-in-law. I felt it would avoid the inevitable chaos and panic his illness would cause at home. The hype and media attention which it attracted only added to everyone's anxiety, including his. Incidentally, the reference to 'Salvador' in the letter was Michael's way of cheering both of us up. It was the code which he used to refer to his physical desire for me. Every time he wrote to me in those years he referred to 'Salvador'. He also signed his letters and various cards and notes with the figure '8'. He was always afraid that someone might intercept our mail and it is a secret I have kept until now. But I only reveal it to illustrate an aspect of our relationship and the lengths to which we went to keep our secret. There was nothing sordid or sleazy about our love life. Those letters are among my most cherished memories of him.

When news that Michael was ill with cancer came out there was intense media and public interest. Tears, prayers and a lot of negativity filled the atmosphere in our little world. He was scared but accepting of his illness and, for everyone's sake, put on a typically optimistic attitude. Because of the attention it attracted I had to take a back seat. I would not dare do anything which raised eyebrows about the extent of our relationship. It was very painful. He underwent the operation and then a severe treatment of radio-iodine. His doctors gave him three years to live and, if he was lucky, between five and ten.

But he made a great recovery and came on in leaps and bounds. He went out and bought himself a new car to show how hopeful he was that he was going to ride out the storm. He also refused to give up smoking. That was when he decided to grow his famous bushy beard. Three years later, Michael buried the doctor who originally said he had three years to live. He often remarked about it, although he was in no way disrespectful to the man's memory. To Michael it was a testimony to the power of God. It was His decision in the end whether you lived or died and disease did not have a say in the matter.

The doctors also informed him that he was lucky he wasn't a 'young married man' because the cancer treatment was likely to render him sterile. He often joked about that, although I used to think about our first son whom I would never see again and his comments that there would be more children. But his recovery was my main concern. His condition was checked every three months and, as time went on, every six months and longer until he showed the signs of full recovery. For the rest of his life he had to take special medication, a substitute drug for his thyroid, which caused problems from time to time. Overall he was more energetic than ever and was soon back to normal in his hectic life as a hard-working priest and performer – and a secret lover and partner. I didn't think much about his sterility after that. I was just glad to see him alive and well. After all, we were going with the flow, like two autumn leaves being carried on a fast-flowing stream with no control of where they would end up.

CHAPTER FIVE

Our Son, Ross

WHEN MICHAEL FULLY recovered from his illness life was very happy in Ballyfermot. It brought us closer together and our relationship blossomed – even if it was behind closed doors. During the day he was the dedicated priest and I was his able assistant and housekeeper. At night we snuggled up together in bed and cuddled. We made love with the same frequency as any other couple. Michael always wanted it more than I did because I could have lived my life without sex. But I gradually lost the inhibitions which had caused such problems during our marathon efforts to consummate this extraordinary relationship, although I could never be described as sexually liberated by any means.

From time to time I still had difficulties with the hypocrisy of the situation we were in. Although we were probably happier in Ballyfermot than anywhere else during our lives together, I suffered perennial bouts of depression prompted by pangs of guilt. I also lived in fear to the point of paranoia that there was gossip about the young housekeeper living with the colourful priest. I often wished that I looked older so as not to attract attention.

In February 1976, my sister Yvonne and her husband, Joe Brogna, an Italian-American, came over for a month's holiday from the States. They stayed in Ballyfermot with us. Joe was a lot like Michael and they got on very well together. They both shared a love of gambling and they owned racehorses. Joe also owned a few bars and was quite well off. My sister Trish, who was in between flats in Dublin, was also staying with us. My sisters had known our secret for some time and they treated Michael like an in-law. He was very comfortable with that. In fact, whenever we were with friends or family who knew about us he appeared more relaxed than normal. For me that illustrated that he really didn't want to live a lie, that deep down he wished that we could be open about our love for each other.

When they were around, Michael was never shy about showing his affection for me. He would often lift me up in front of them and kiss me. They were very happy times. One evening we were all watching TV in the sitting-room when Michael decided to go to bed around 10.30 p.m. He winked at me, which was a hint that he wanted me to go with him. Shortly afterwards I said good night to everyone and flippantly joked, 'I'm going to make a baby', and everyone laughed. That night we made love.

A few weeks later Michael and I went out with Yvonne, Trish and Joe to the Green Isle Hotel for dinner. I was ravenous with hunger, which was highly unusual for me because I never had much of an appetite. After the meal I suddenly felt very ill in my stomach and was sick in the toilet. In the previous week or so I had felt strange. Something made me suspect that there was a baby growing inside me but I reckoned that was impossible because Michael had been told that the cancer treatment could make him sterile. While Michael and Joe got stuck into talking about horses I whispered my fears to Trish. She suggested that she would take a urine sample to the Coombe maternity hospital on my behalf to see if I was in fact pregnant.

She was to call me a week later, on 28 February, the day of my birthday, with the results. I tried not to think too much about it and didn't tell Michael. That day, Joe wanted to go into town to see Moore Street and its colourful fruit and vegetable stalls. We spent much of that afternoon browsing, although I was anxious to get home for the call – and the good or bad news. Unfortunately, with the way I felt, I didn't know which result would be good or bad!

When we got back to Ballyfermot, Michael was home and everything seemed normal. I was nervous and asked if there had been any calls for me. Michael said there hadn't been any. We had brought home some delicious sweet cakes and pastries. I went and made tea and we sat around talking and having a laugh about the market. Afterwards, Yvonne suddenly jumped up and suggested that we both go to the kitchen and wash up. I didn't know what to make of this because, as far as Yvonne was concerned, washing dishes was the least of her priorities. In the kitchen I was filling the sink with water when she stood beside me and put her arm on my shoulder. Then she hit me with the news. Michael had taken the call from Trish and told her. I was pregnant.

At first I was in a state of shock and it didn't really sink in. I laughed when I realised that this was Yvonne's reason for being suddenly so house proud. Then several thoughts began racing around in my mind. I was dumbfounded and couldn't believe I was pregnant because I thought Michael was sterile. I was also on the pill to control my periods and the bad premenstrual tension I suffered. And I had not been with any other man apart from Michael. Then I remembered what he said the day I signed away Michael Ivor, that 'there will be more children down the road'. I felt that this child had been sent to us by God because He wanted us to have a family. At the same time I was scared of what would happen and how we would deal with the situation. Michael, I knew, did not want children. But at the same time he wanted to be with me and continue to be a priest. I felt a cold, familiar chill run through my body. I was entering another darkened tunnel and only God knew where the end would be.

When I came out of the kitchen the atmosphere in the room had become subdued. My eyes met Michael's across the plume of smoke rising from his cigarette. Both of us were stunned. That night we all got ready and went out for a meal to celebrate my birthday. There was no more discussion or mention of pregnancy. For the time being at least the subject was put on hold. I now knew why I had such an uncharacteristic appetite. During the meal Michael cracked jokes at me about how much I was eating. I smiled across the table at him. He always made fun when he was trying to hide his apprehension.

It may seem bizarre and hard to understand but neither of us discussed it for over a week while Yvonne and Joe were staying. Even though we were alone together, sleeping in the same bed, we avoided the issue. The enormity of the consequences pushed us into a state of denial. It was like nothing was wrong. When our visitors had returned to the States we talked about it briefly but no plans were mentioned. Neither of us was happy. He was scared and kept his thoughts to himself. He thought that he couldn't make me pregnant. But following the adoption he knew he couldn't suggest to me that I also give up this child.

In his subconscious I thought Michael was happy with the pregnancy. Maybe I was picking up the wrong signals. In the final months of the pregnancy, when we were alone, he would gently stroke my bump and murmur things like: 'Imagine . . . there is part of me growing in there.' Then he would place his head on my tummy, listening for movement. Perhaps I was deluding myself that this would be plain sailing. But there were special times during that nine months that were a diversion from having to consider the few, unpalatable options open to us. For the time being the future was being put on hold. We were just going with the flow. Like the leaves in the fast-running stream, we realised we had no control over our destiny. Everything was in God's hands.

During those months we went on as normal. We slept

together and made love but avoided discussing our problem even though it was foremost in our minds. My brain was racing all the time during those tortuous months. I suffered terrible stomachaches and was nauseous most of the time. In May, Michael travelled to Australia as a guest of the Irish community. He performed his show in the Sydney Opera House. During the weeks he was away there were few visitors calling to the house and it gave me some time to think. Trish called around regularly and did my shopping for me and I stayed in most of the time. I knew that whatever happened I was determined not to give up this baby. In one way I was happy that I was pregnant. I wanted to fill the vacuum left in my heart by the loss of my first child, who was never out of my thoughts. I was also deeply in love with the father of my child. If I hadn't been in a forbidden relationship then everything would have been blissfully normal. But I had to hide the pregnancy because of the scandal and speculation it would cause. In fact, I didn't see a gynaecologist until I was six months pregnant. Michael was no longer giving refuge to unmarried mothers who could provide camouflage like before. It was the easy way out not to face the grim realities and reach a decision.

In June I went on holiday to Yvonne and Joe in America. The weather was sweltering and it was dreadfully uncomfortable being pregnant. On the way back to Ireland I visited my sister Maria and her husband, Dave, until the end of July. All the time I was away Michael wrote and called me on the phone regularly. But there was never any conversation about the one subject which was foremost in our minds – our baby. When it was time for me to travel back to Dublin I was extremely nervous. I was six months pregnant and beginning to show. We were to take an evening flight from Heathrow so that it would be dark on arrival. I felt more comfortable arriving under cover of darkness. However, there was a heavy fog over the airport and we were informed that the planes were unable to take off. The airline put us up in a hotel and around 6 a.m. the next morning we were called and told our flight could take off. When I arrived back in Dublin it couldn't have been brighter. There was a clear blue sky and hot sunshine, the last thing I wanted. I looked bloody stupid wearing a big raincoat shuffling through the arrivals hall when everyone else was in shortsleeves.

Maria and Dave stayed for a few days and then returned home. Michael informed me that he had made arrangements for me to spend the remainder of my pregnancy in Limerick living with Peg O'Connell, a doctor who was a close friend of his. I had known Peg for some years, she was a kind, charitable woman and we were quite friendly. Michael drove me to Limerick in late August. I hated every mile of that journey, I was like a fugitive running away. I did not want to go because I wanted to stay with Michael, although I knew there was no alternative. Peg made me welcome. She lived in a big rambling house called 'Elmhurst' which was used as flats for doctors. I had a room to myself. It was almost too big and made the single bed look tiny. It had bare floorboards and was sparsely furnished. I had my own kettle and tea and coffee. I spent a lot of time alone in that room when Peg was off working. She did her best to make me feel comfortable and welcome but I couldn't help feeling depressed and lonely. The most enjoyable time there was when Peg took me off for a few days to the annual Merriman Summer School in Ennis, County Clare. We had a great time.

Michael rang me regularly and came down to visit as often as he could. He made plans to come one Sunday but never showed up. As evening turned into night and there was not even a phone call, I was distressed and worried. It turned out that one of the other curates had to go off at short notice and Michael had to fill in for him. I began attending a gynaecologist in Limerick shortly after I arrived. Peg made the appointment for me. He was a very nice man and his surgery was near the train station. When I visited him I often took the train to Dublin where I stayed overnight in an apartment owned by Peg. She gave me the key. Michael would come over from Ballyfermot and visit. We used to hold each other and talk about things but still didn't discuss what was going to happen when I had the baby.

Even though I was only there for a few months, the time in Limerick seemed to drag on forever. I went over my due date by a few days and my doctor decided to induce me. On the morning of 3 November, at 8.30 a.m., Peg brought me to the Limerick Regional Hospital. I was put on a drip and after four hours of labour, at 2.25 p.m., I gave birth to our son Ross. He was a big baby and weighed 8 lb 4 oz. He was bigger than Michael Ivor, long and leggy, with equally long arms. He had very long hair for a baby, which curled at the nape of his neck, with a long grey streak on the left side of his head which is his birthmark. It is similar to a birthmark one of Michael's nephews has.

I stayed in hospital for a week. Michael came with a friend to collect me. He was bright and cheery, although I knew he was trying hard not to show his pride. Michael would not allow himself to develop a bond with his son because he was too scared of the consequences and the heartache it might cause him. Things began to move so fast from that moment and Michael resumed control of my life. He had made arrangements for Ross to be cared for in Madonna House in Dublin by the nuns. He convinced me that it was the best place for him to be cared for while we worked out what to do next. Then, on the way back to Dublin, I got another surprise – my son's christening had been hastily arranged, again without my being consulted. Our son was christened Ross McDaid in a church in Borris-in-Ossory in a simple Babygro and wrapped in a crocheted tablecloth.

When the ceremony was over we continued on our journey to Dublin. It was late in the evening when we arrived at Madonna House where Ross was to remain for a month. Just as in the case of our first child everything was happening faster than I could think. Michael had made his mind up that I was not going to have this child either. The protection of his career was more important and he wanted to run away from his responsibilities. Again I had that familiar feeling of emptiness and sadness. I hated leaving my little baby in that place and going back home to Ballyfermot pretending that nothing had happened, maintaining a false image at any cost. I cried all the way back to the house. Michael just looked at the road ahead and remained quiet.

Over the next few days I made several tearful pleas to him to get Ross out of that place. Michael called a nurse he knew and she agreed to foster him. I visited my baby every day until I felt that situation was no longer satisfactory. He contacted infantile excema and a neighbour of a friend agreed to foster him instead. The woman was fantastic with the baby and he thrived. But I could only go to visit my child when all I wanted was to bring him home and rear him myself. Michael was in a quandary over the situation himself and we had several flaming rows as the weeks dragged into months. The rows became a daily occurrence between us and grew in intensity. I again found myself drifting along and getting no answers or support from the man who had asked me to share marriage vows with him.

He wanted me to stay with him and put Ross up for adoption. I wanted him to make a decision to either leave the priesthood or let Ross and me go our own way. When it came to that he had a catchall answer for me: 'What will I do if I leave, I can't do anything else.' Michael always had a happy knack of not addressing an issue. He could close up and not say anything. I was incensed that he was quite happy that our son was out of the way while I, the woman he claimed to love, was pining for him around the clock. He kept repeating 'We will work something out' over and over until it sounded like a bad record. Then I decided to write a letter to Michael's father telling him about our relationship and Ross. I also told Michael that I was going to tell the parish priest and would mail the letter on the way.

Michael didn't believe me and called my bluff. I posted the letter and went to see the priest although he wasn't at home. When I went back to the house Michael flew into an almost uncontrollable rage. He screamed and cursed at me for sending the letter, he couldn't believe that I could do that. As the row got worse I said that I had had enough and I began to pack. Michael cooled down and tried to stop me. Again he said he would try to sort something out. That was the final straw. There was a pantry in the house. I swung open the door and swept all the china off the shelves, sending it crashing across the floor. I stood trembling in a rage with tears flooding down my face. 'I am not your housekeeper, Michael, I am your wife . . . that was what you wanted. Now I want to have our child, I am not letting Ross go the same as the last just so that you can keep your cosy little life. You have controlled me for long enough and now I'm getting out,' the tears came almost as fast and furious as the words. Michael again tried to assuage me. We cried together and made up. Later we went to bed together. But despite the tenderness between us I had made up my mind.

The next morning Michael left the house at the crack of dawn and went to his family home in Blanchardstown to wait for the postman. I will never know if he actually intercepted the letter or if his father got it or not. It was now late June 1977, one of the hottest summers on record. I looked up the papers and eventually found a job advertised in Boston. A priest friend of my family interviewed me in the Gresham Hotel in Dublin and I got the job, taking care of an elderly stroke patient. It was the kind of job I had always been good at. I decided to go ahead and get set up and then bring Ross with me to his new home. I took him out of the foster home and asked my sister Peggy (whom Michael didn't know) if she would look after him while I was gone. She was one of my sisters who had no idea about my relationship with Michael. She was happy to oblige.

Michael was not pleased at all. He did not want me to go

and he didn't know where Ross was going so he wouldn't be able to see him. But I was firm in my mind, he could not have it every way. In September I flew out to Boston, where I was met by my employer, Karen Clarke. I was to look after her grandfather, a lovely old man they called Gramps. I was terrified of being out there on my own but my determination to get a life made me persevere. The family lived in a big house in Winchester and I had my own room upstairs. She was vice-president of a company and her husband, Tommy, a public relations consultant. That night they took me out along with her mother for dinner and then to a local production of the musical, *Fiddler on the Roof*. I had almost a week to get the run of the house and get to know everyone in the family. Gramps was still in hospital and I went to see him every day so that he got used to me. I also learned the physiotherapy which I had to do with him daily.

When he came out of hospital I was initially nervous, but that soon passed and he was a joy to nurse most of the time. I got on wonderfully and was treated like one of the family. In a few weeks I had settled into a routine. On my nights off I signed up for college and took up shorthand and typing. Other times I visited my sister Yvonne and her family who lived 20 miles from Winchester. The Clarkes were also making efforts to secure a green card for me so that I could work legitimately without the fear of deportation. I was due to get it sometime around March or April of 1978 and was so excited at the prospect. Karen Clarke became very much like a sister to me.

I called home a few times every week to see how Ross was doing. I couldn't wait for the time when we would finally be reunited as mother and son and get on with our lives. I felt so cheated and angry that I had to be separated from him at all. I was also desperately missing Michael. He rang every Thursday. He also wrote to me and sent taped messages and told me how lonely he was without me. I still have some of those letters. One of them read:

Dear Phyllis,

After your phone call last night I decided to scrap the letter and tape most of the news and include this note with it.

The place here is bloody lonely and I wouldn't mind even to hear you giving out. You'll never know how important the gifts you left me are. I leave them where I can see them when I'm not using them and they give me a sense of your presence. You know I haven't got a good photo of you? Send me one on – preferably one of you grinning with the wrinkles at your eyes and any other personal items that you think I'd like. Maybe also some personal instructions that will replace the orders you gave when you were here. I left your pills notice on the wall and, believe it or not, I am washing my teeth every day for you. Sounds silly, I know, but it's like something for love. I do it for you and it's a time for thinking of you.

On second thoughts I'll send this note separately in case the tape is slower in the post. Skippy is a bit lost, Barbie [*both our dogs*] is still chasing the cars and Salvador is driving me mad since you left. He misses you terribly.

Love Michael.

P.S. Apart from the letters with news send me a nice one that I keep and read when I'm lonely, which is all the time.

Many mornings I woke up on a pillow saturated with tears. I wanted so badly to be with him again. But I had set out to make a life for us, if Michael wanted to be part of that life then the decision was his, he knew what he had to do.

I got friendly with a pal of Karen and Tommy, called Gary. He had a share in a rock club and we all used to go there on Thursday nights after Michael phoned. One Thursday evening Gary was in hurry and I had to go when Michael hadn't called. When he did phone he was told that I had gone out with a guy. But there was absolutely nothing going on between Gary and me. We were just friends and, anyway, a relationship was the last thing on my mind. The next night Michael called and he quizzed me for ages about this guy Gary. I could see that he was concerned and maybe jealous.

The hardest time in Boston was on Ross's first birthday and I was very upset. Karen got her mother to look after Gramps and she and Tommy took me out to dinner to cheer me up. They were looking forward to me bringing Ross over to live. I found it hard not to cry in front of them. About six weeks before Christmas I put together a big box of goodies for Ross and his cousins. I spent Thanksgiving with Yvonne and her family. It was a nice day, just like Christmas but without Santa Claus or gifts. Michael rang and was brief. He said that he was thinking of contacting Peggy because he wanted to see Ross. I pleaded with him not to, because she might suspect that he was more than a concerned priest. I could see that it would only make things complicated for everyone.

On Christmas Eve I went out with Karen and Tommy and we spent until 4 a.m. in the morning at a party in their friend's house. We had to get up early because there were 35 people coming to the house for Christmas dinner. I went to 11.30 a.m. Mass and went back for dinner. I remember we had roast beef, which wasn't much of a Christmas dinner as far as I was concerned. The house was crammed with people, all of them enjoying themselves. It was hard to find a quiet corner to give in to the loneliness in my heart. I thought about little Ross playing under the tree back at home and Michael saying Mass in Ballyfermot before going for his Christmas dinner alone. I couldn't wait for the day to be over.

The next day I went to Yvonne's and took gifts to everyone. Then it was back to work and I was glad to have my mind taken off things. New Year's Eve was another lonely day. There wasn't a phone call from Michael and that made it worse. That night I fell asleep on the couch and missed the ringing in of 1978. I went to bed and cried myself to sleep. I wondered what kind of year was in store for me. On New Year's Day I did the bits and pieces I had to do in the house and Karen drove me to Yvonne's house. I was going to stay overnight and go out with her and Joe.

In the early evening I heard the key turning in the front door. Joe walked in and right on his heels there was Michael, with that big beaming smile on his face. 'Happy New Year everyone . . . God bless you all,' he said in a typically cheerful voice. I was stunned to silence for about ten seconds. Hearing his voice warmed my heart. I jumped up and raced into his arms. He lifted me off the ground and gave me a big tight hug. We were with Joe and Yvonne and there was no reason for caution. I had to pinch myself to make sure I wasn't dreaming. We all had tea and pie and talked for a while. Joe drove us back to Winchester, where I proudly introduced Michael to everyone else in my life in Boston. They were aware that he was a priest but no one cared to pry into our affairs. Karen cooked one of her Cordon Bleu specials for dinner. When Gramps was settled in for the night, Karen and Tommy went out to give us some space and time together. We sat together on the couch, kissing and hugging. I still couldn't believe he was there.

He sat back in the couch with his hands behind his head like he was at home. I asked him where everyone at home thought he was.

'Oh, I told them I was going to Scotland for a few days,' he replied with a crafty smile.

'Jesus, what happens if you have an accident or something and they find out that you are here, how will you explain that?' I asked in a slight fuss.

'Don't be worrying about that – let's just enjoy ourselves for now,' he reassured me.

Then I asked him about wanting to go to see Ross. When he said he had visited our son, I was angry because of the difficulties that could cause. I would be proved right.

'I just couldn't stand it anymore, that we are all split up . . . I just wanted to see him,' Michael confessed.

I did not respond, my heart sank down to my toes. My feelings were so confused. 'Is this the man who did everything in his power to have Ross adopted?' I asked myself. I was so glad that he was here with me but afraid of the future. But there was nothing I could do about it just then so I decided to put my worries on hold and enjoy the few days he had with me. We slept together and made love. It was so nice feeling him next to me again. Karen and Tommy gave me as much time off as I needed to be with Michael. He hired a car the next day and we did some touring and shopping and went for meals. America is such a big, uncomplicated place compared to Ireland and we didn't feel the need to hide our feelings for one another. But the days went like hours and I dreaded his departure. We had such a wonderful, intimate time together, away from prying eyes and interruptions.

* * *

I was very lonely when he was gone and I was afraid of the consequences of Michael's visit to Ross. My fears were justified a few days later when a letter with familiar handwriting arrived in the mail. It was from my mother. I couldn't believe the words I read. It was a tirade of abuse and outrage aimed at me. She called me a tramp, a hussy, a whore, every abusive name under the sun. Someone had somehow let it slip to her about Michael, Ross and I. My mother was a fanatical Catholic all her life who neither drank nor smoked. She was a daily Mass-goer, a woman who sent money and donations all over the world to help with the education of young priests. She was angry and disgusted that I had a child by a priest, a man of God.

In the letter she threatened going to the newspapers and the bishops, and even the Pope, to expose what she called our 'evil' relationship, which to her was nothing more than the influence of Satan himself. I was gripped by sheer panic. There was also anger at her for her harsh words. How dare this woman, who had never been much of a parent to us, cast judgement on me and my life. If it hadn't been for the utter mess which was her and dad's marriage I would not have been in this situation in the first place. I decided that there was nothing to do but get on a plane and go home to sort out this mess. 'If only Michael had kept his nose out and stayed away this wouldn't be happening,' I thought. His actions were preventing us having a life without him. The part of him which loved us was overruling his need for self-preservation.

When I told Karen that I had to leave, she was furious. I couldn't blame her because they had done so much for me and now I was suddenly leaving them in the lurch. But there was nothing I could do about it. I wanted to kill Michael for not listening to me and for ruining everything. Karen fired me on the spot and did not want me to work out my notice. So I got a cab over to Yvonne's house.

I tried to call Michael several times but there was no reply on his phone. I had saved money from my work over the previous five months and was lucky to catch a flight to Ireland the following day. I got Michael just before I flew out of Boston. He was pretty upset and worried about my mother finding out. 'I wish now I had listened to you, Phyl, I guess I was being selfish,' he sighed.

'Let's just hope that it's not too late,' I snapped back angrily and hung up. Michael was waiting for me at the airport and drove me back to Ballyfermot. Unexpectedly, the place wasn't in too much of a mess but the state of the place was not my worry. I calmed myself before going to face my mother.

I went to her house in Phibsboro and she was there alone. I don't recall where my father was at the time. She began saying the same venomous remarks she had written in her letter. It was as if she had been rehearsing the tirade for weeks. She screamed and ranted at me. Then she pointed out some prophecy which stated that priests would lead souls to hell. I began to get angry at her. How dare she compare our love to some kind of evil. Ross was not the product of anything evil. Then she asked the extraordinary question: 'How could the holy ordained hands of a priest touch a woman?' Those words made me feel like dirt. I replied: 'Mammy, it is you who are flying in the face of God. You're supposed to be a religious woman, well, God made us in his own likeness and image, so how can any of us be dirty?' She began to calm down and the anger in her face turned to sadness. 'I suppose you're right.' I pleaded with her not to do anything which would harm Ross. She agreed.

We had tea in virtual silence. Normally a mother and daughter would have something to talk about if they hadn't seen each other for several months. Not us. I felt that I had averted disaster for all three of us by winning her silence. Since Michael's death I have often wondered if her angry outburst was her way of expressing her fears for me. Things have happened which perhaps justify her fears. As soon as I could, I went to see my little son. When I saw him my heart leaped. He was a gorgeous child. He had rosy red cheeks and a lovely little smile. I just wanted to grab him and take him away with me. But I knew that it wasn't yet possible and I had to be patient until I sorted everything out. On my return to Ballyfermot Michael was waiting. He was anxious to know what had happened. I told him everything and broke down and cried: 'Now do you see what you have done? You have messed up our chances of a life in America. You have involved my mother in something she doesn't need to know and I only hope to God she doesn't go ahead with her threats.'

Michael looked sheepish and replied: 'I'm sorry. I was so lonely with you so far away. I just had to see Ross.'

'Well, you are a very selfish man. Just when I am about to sort out a life for myself you go and mess things up big time,' I snapped back, refusing to fall for his persuasive charm.

'Don't worry, I will go and see your mother and sort things out,' he promised.

A few weeks later he did go to see her but I was never told what transpired between them. No doubt he used his inimitable priestly charm. But after that my mother appeared to grow fonder of Michael and she adored Ross. On a number of occasions in later life she asked him to leave the priesthood and take us, his family, away and make a life for all three of us. But Michael managed to either divert the conversation or charm his way out of it.

Over the following months Michael decided that the best solution was for him to buy a house on the north side of the city. I think he wanted Ross and me at a safe distance but always within reach when he wanted to be with us. Again, he was having it his own way. The house was renovated and just before Ross and I were about to move in the local residents association got wind that Michael was the owner. He was well known for his help to young pregnant women and they sent him a letter saying they did not want unmarried mothers in the area.

So he sold that house and bought another on Bayview Avenue in the North Strand area of the city. This house also had to be renovated for us. During this period I was staying with Michael as before and Ross was with Peggy. But she understandably grew impatient at the situation and felt that I was leaving Ross with her just to facilitate my precarious lifestyle. In late April she called me and insisted that I begin looking after Ross. I had no choice, although the house on Bayview was not ready for habitation. The only place we could go, suggested Michael, was back to Ballyfermot. And there we were, all three of us together under the one roof despite all the efforts we had made to ensure otherwise.

In one sense I was delighted that fate had thrown us together. It was as if we had never been apart. Overnight Michael developed a close bond with his son. It was beautiful to watch. When we were alone he was the doting dad. And while he was always around for what Ross called 'hugs and bugs' I can't recall him ever changing a nappy or making a bottle. But despite our new-found happiness, I was also apprehensive at the kind of reception we would get from parishioners and the other curates in the parish. There was bound to have been curiosity and rumours about the disappearances of the housekeeper, but Michael reassured me with the words: 'Sure they can only speculate.'

Then one day, a local woman, who subsequently became my friend, arrived at the door and introduced herself to me. Then she asked: 'Who is this little boy?' I felt my gut tightening at the question. 'That's Ross.' Then came the crunch. 'Ross who?' Before I could think my mouth replied for me: 'Ross Hamilton, he's my son.' From that moment on we became Hamilton. In a way it was perfect. Now the people in the parish assumed that I had gone off to be married in America, had a child and was now divorced. Not unexpectedly, Michael thought it was a great idea. We eventually changed our names by deed poll and Michael made out a baptism certificate for Ross in that name when it was time for him to go to school.

I could not suppress the worries I had about speculation concerning myself and Ross and the damage it could do to Michael. I suggested that it would be better for us to move into a flat on the north side of the city until the renovations at Bayview were completed. Michael helped me search for a flat and we found one on the Howth Road. It was a garden flat and would be perfect for a month or so while we were waiting. Again fate stepped in. Everything that could go wrong went wrong. First the electricity broke down on a few occasions and the place was infested with mice. Then we were flooded and the floor coverings had to be removed. After the flooding there was a break in the water supply. Michael said that the place was no place for his son and he brought us back again to Ballyfermot.

We began to live together as a family, even though it was not what we planned. Despite the continued secrecy I began to feel comfortable. In my wildest dreams I had not thought that I would be living under the one roof with my man and my son. Michael seemed really happy, too, and acted the role of the husband and father. He doted on Ross. When people would come into the house and compliment me on my beautiful son it used to get to him that he couldn't take the credit. When we were alone together he would say: 'You can take the credit for being his mother and I can't say anything even though I want to.'

After a while we just seemed to settle in together as a family and there no longer seemed to be a need to move to Bayview. Like everything else, it just happened. There was never any more mention about it and Michael used it for young married couples as a place where they could stay while waiting to buy their own homes. The parishioners seemed to accept us without question again. No one asked me about my personal life and the cover story just seemed to stick. The other children came to play with Ross and he went to their houses. His second birthday was one of the most special moments with my little boy. On his first I cried myself asleep 3,000 miles away from him and his father. Now we were all together. Michael played host and there were over 20 kids. He loved children and they gravitated towards him.

From the moment we started living together Ross never wanted for anything. Michael spoiled the child rotten and let him do what he wanted which was to lead to serious problems between us when our son became a teenager. If Michael was away with the *All Priests' Show* or on holiday, he couldn't wait to get home. If he came in late he would creep up to Ross's bedroom and look in on him and stroke his head. Our first Christmas together was the most memorable and happiest of my life. Michael went out and bought the biggest tree he could find and he bought Ross enough toys and gadgets to fill an entire store. Michael ensured that holidays from school were full of boyish excitement and took his son everywhere.

Shortly after his second birthday Michael insisted on bringing me down to claim the Single Parent's Allowance. I didn't want to because I felt it was dishonest and we had a big blazing argument. 'You are entitled to it and that is why you are going to claim it,' he insisted, adding: 'I have a family but I am paying tax as a single man so you might as well benefit from it.' I hated collecting that money through the years. In my mind the last thing I was, was an unmarried mother. I had the most wonderful husband in the world.

Michael brought Ross to school on his first day. He went off holding his son by the hand. It must have been a strange sight. I often got angry at the thought that people probably looked at him as being a charitable man, helping out a poor unmarried wretch of a mother. He brought Ross into his classroom and put him in his chair. Through the years Ross blossomed into a beautiful young boy and he and his father became inseparable.

There were plenty of little ups and downs in the following five or six years. As Ross grew older, Michael and I decided to no longer sleep together for fear that it might confuse him. We always ensured that in the mornings we were in our own beds. Throughout his life Ross called Michael, 'Father'. One day he came in from playing very upset. One of the other kids told him that he couldn't call Michael his father because he was a priest. I wouldn't tell Ross who his father was until he was old enough but somehow Ross instinctively knew the secret. Like everything else in our bizarre lives Ross and Michael lived together and loved each other as father and son without openly acknowledging the fact.

CHAPTER SIX

My Attacker

MICHAEL'S POPULARITY AS a priest grew while we were in Ballyfermot. The highlight of his fame was in 1979 when he and his old friend Eamonn Casey were the main 'warm-up men' for the Pope's youth Mass in Galway during his autumn visit. There had been an incredible fuss and Michael was so excited when he got the news that he had been chosen to address the crowd. He was brilliant and the half million or so young people of Ireland enjoyed him – perhaps even more than the Pope himself. His winning way was that he was a man of the people who could communicate with everyone on his or her own level, unlike so many priests today who are supercilious, condescending and didactic. It was Michael's ultimate performance and it consolidated his position as a household name. Coupled with his dedicated hard work as a curate, this earned him the notice of the hierarchy who inevitably promoted him to parish priest. In fact, he was the first of his classmates in the seminary to achieve the rank. But with that came instability and another period of upheaval for the three of us as a family unit.

He was again placed in a huge, sprawling working-class suburb, this time Finglas South on the north-west edge of the city. Again it was an extremely challenging appointment with a high rate of unemployment and poverty. I was uneasy about being uprooted from Ballyfermot. We had settled down as a family and we were all very happy there. Ross was going to school and had friends. Our house had a warm, homely atmosphere.

Although I was delighted for him, I was sad for Ross and me. The move created a lot of tension in our relationship. We rowed regularly about small, inconsequential things, when in fact the rows were the manifestation of our concerns for the future. I had grown to accept the situation of living two lives, with Michael as a curate. It was tolerable and an equal balance between his role as a priest and that of partner and parent. During the years in Ballyfermot with Ross we had grown closer as a family and it seemed as if we would never again be apart.

Now, suddenly, Mother Church was grabbing hold of him and dragging him away from us. It was clear that his devotion to the Church was stronger than to us, although Michael refused to see it that way. In one sense he could not have turned down the appointment but it made him uncomfortable and apprehensive for the future of the secret side of his life. In the months before the move to Finglas a wedge had been driven between us.

We were due to move in June 1983. The previous month was so busy that it provided a distraction from the worries and anxieties for the future. Ross received his First Holy Communion on the 21st of the month and just over a week later Michael held his silver jubilee celebration Mass as a priest. It was a proud day for both Michael and me, but particularly Michael, who presided over his son's special ceremony. I spent weeks planning for Ross's big day. I decided to dress him as close to white as possible. It took me a lot of time and effort, but I eventually found a little off-white suit, creak shirt, brown tie and handkerchief and cream shoes. Michael gave Ross his own communion medal which he placed on a rosette.

A shared moment in a photo booth on a day-trip to Bundoran,
Co. Donegal, 1976.

This picture of us was taken in the back garden of the house in Ballyfermot where we lived together from the early 1970s.

With Michael when he paid a surprise visit to me in Boston, New Year's Day, 1978.

Michael and Ross together as father and son. Every moment he had spare, Michael spent with Ross.

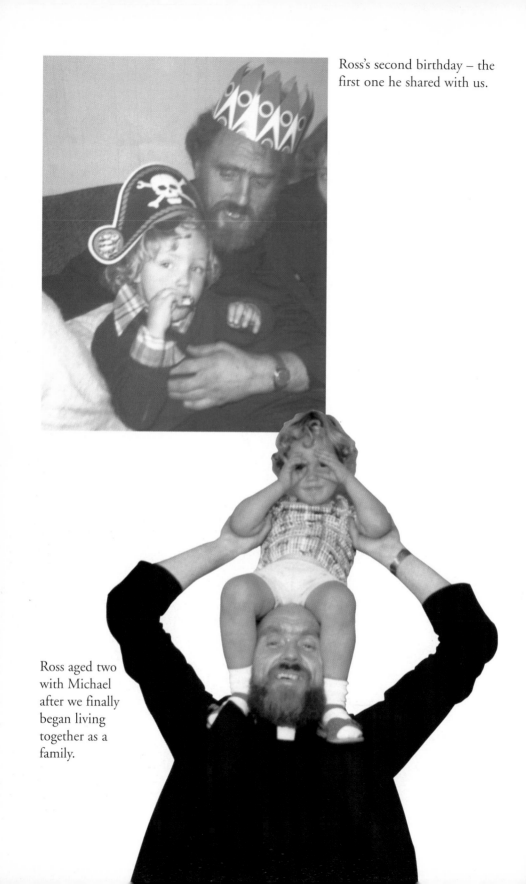

Ross's second birthday – the first one he shared with us.

Ross aged two with Michael after we finally began living together as a family.

Ross and Michael in 1979.

Michael with Eamonn Casey photographed during the Pope's visit to Galway. At that time their secret lives were unknown to the public.
(*Connacht Tribune*)

Hallowe'en and Ross's eighth birthday: Michael gave him a watch.

Michael and Ross after we had moved to Harold's Cross.

Happy times: Michael and me in the kitchen of the house in Mount Harold Terrace before the Eamonn Casey affair became public.

Ross with his father prior to setting off for the Feile rock festival in Tipperary.

The final family photograph taken the morning before Michael entered hospital for tests.

Ross and I must now adjust to life without Michael – the father and lover we will never forget.

I had trouble finding an outfit for myself which I liked but eventually I did. I remember Michael looking at me when I tried it on and he smiled and said: 'God, but you're a real cracker in that.' On the morning of Ross's communion, the three of us were busy getting ready. Michael helped get Ross ready. Unfortunately, the child was only six and a half years old, probably too young to realise how special the day was. Just as we were about to go out to the car for the journey to the church, Ross made an astonishing announcement. He said that he did not want me to go to the church with him because I was 'just a little mammy'. I couldn't believe my ears. He had often heard Michael refer to me as that but only in affectionate terms, but Ross had his own interpretation. 'All the other mammies are big and you are too small,' he declared with a frown on his face and his hands on his hips. Michael winked at me and smiled. He got down on his hunkers and rubbed his son's golden curly hair. 'Ah, don't worry, Ross, sure they'll think that she is your big sister.' Ross considered Michael's suggestion for a few moments and then looked at me. He was satisfied with that and we all headed for the church.

Michael concelebrated the Mass with a few other priests and my mother, sister and a few friends came for the day. A guy who was outside the church with a mobile video unit offered to make a tape for us, which was great to have even if it was a pretty amateurish effort. Even the church was almost full. I could see only one child there that morning, Ross. Every now and then I caught Michael's eye as he watched his little boy from the altar. I could see how proud he was as Ross stepped up to receive the communion. Michael couldn't help smiling as he watched his son stepping up to the altar. After the ceremony and the pictures, Michael drove us all back to the house where we had a big breakfast. Then we went for the inevitable tour of friends' and relations' houses. A week later we went to the children's Mass which Michael celebrated. We had no breakfast because we had to fast. When we came out of the church Ross turned to me and said: 'Mammy, let's hurry home to have something to eat, all I've had is that bread they give you at Mass . . . I'm starving.' When I told Michael he thought it was hilarious.

The following week was Michael's silver jubilee celebration. He celebrated Mass in the church in Blanchardstown in front of his family and friends and afterwards there was a huge party for over 700 guests. A special marquee was set up in the grounds of St Brigid's GAA club, where he had once played with distinction. It had a full bar and caterers brought in food. It was a very well-organised affair. I was given a group to look after and I remember I was busy all day. It was a splendid party and went on into the early hours of the morning.

Then came the day we had both been dreading – the move to Rivermount Parish in Finglas. The presbytery was a tiny, pre-fabricated bungalow with two small bedrooms, a small kitchen, sitting-room and a modest bathroom. The walls were like cardboard and Ross had to sleep on a fold-up bed at the base of Michael's. There wasn't enough room for all the furniture and belongings we had painstakingly packed back in Ballyfermot. Most of the stuff had to be stored in a garage. Compared to our previous home this one was bleak. Ross was lonesome for his friends in Ballyfermot and Michael tried to compensate by bringing them over to Finglas and taking Ross over to their houses. He tried to console me by saying that we would not have to stay there for long. I began considering moving again. I felt that I couldn't live there and decided that I would help get him set up first.

I planned to go to the US again in yet another attempt to start a new life. It was a tough decision to make. When I told Michael he was very upset. 'You can't go, you can't take Ross away from me,' he said almost in tears. It broke my heart, but I explained that now he was a parish priest I found it more difficult to go on living our lie. I agreed to go to America on a trial basis. Ross was enrolled in the local school in September but he only stayed a month. We left for Boston in October.

Michael drove us to the airport. Ross was a bit confused with what was going on. He thought he was going on a holiday but didn't want to leave Michael at home.

We stayed for a while with Yvonne and Joe and then went on to stay with my friend Phyl and her husband in Florida. About ten times a day Ross asked about his father. He was very home-sick and unhappy. 'Please, mum, I want to go home to Father.' Michael called a few times a week and always insisted on speaking with Ross. I could see that he was really missing us, too, and it broke my heart. I was torn between my common sense that told me the nature of my relationship with Michael would never change and my love, which told me to disregard my concerns and go back.

In the meantime, Yvonne was diagnosed as suffering from a disease of the gums and had to go to hospital for emergency surgery. So Ross and I flew back to Boston and I looked after her children for her while she was away. We spent Christmas in Boston and I made every effort so that it was special for Ross. However, we both missed Michael terribly. Shortly after Christmas I got a call to say that my mother had had a heart attack. It was decided that Yvonne would fly home the next day and I stayed to look after the children.

She came back after a week and it was suggested that I should go home to be near my mother in case she grew ill again. I was the only one who had no firm roots. Ross was delighted at the news and couldn't wait to see his father. Neither could I, although I was very apprehensive. I wanted to stay with my mother to look after her. But Michael was on the phone and asked me to come and stay with him. I agreed. As I got on the plane I said to myself: 'God, I hope I am doing the right thing . . . what am I letting myself in for?' It appeared that no matter how many times I attempted to change my life, God intervened and brought me back to the place I was trying to get away from. In the end I threw my hands up to heaven and said: 'OK, God, if this is what you want I won't fight it anymore, I will resume my life with Michael and get on with this crazy life.'

Michael was there in the arrivals hall waiting for us. He didn't hide his delight at seeing us again. Ross ran to him and he lifted him up in his arms and hugged him tightly. He winked at me and smiled, 'Welcome home.' On the way back to the cramped bungalow we stopped off to see my mother. She was making a good recovery and was glad to see us. She and my father were still living together after all the years of turmoil and adversity between them. He was in poor health himself and could not help my mother because he had developed TB and arthritis had twisted up his body. Michael went out and got whatever things she needed. I got my home-coming hug back at the house when Ross was in bed. Ross went back to school in January and life went back to what passed as normality. And there I was again, meandering through life, going with the flow, not knowing where it was taking us. Michael kept reassuring me that within three years we would be moving again. I decided to get stuck into working alongside Michael as I had done in Ballyfermot.

There was a lot of poverty in Finglas and sometimes it was very upsetting for Michael and myself when we saw the extent of the human misery. One night a little boy about 10 years old called to the door looking for Michael who was out somewhere. I asked him how I could help and he asked for a candle. 'Why do you want a candle?' I asked curiously. 'Because we have no light at home,' the little boy replied matter-of-factly. I was in shock and took his name and address. When Michael came home I told him about the boy. He went around to the address to find a deserted mother with five little children. They had no electricity, no cooking facilities, no floor coverings and not even adequate bedding. He was broken hearted by what he found. He was also angry that people were suffering so much. So, in typical fashion he went to work and soon helped the poor woman get her home together. There are a lot of people who can fondly recall how that great man I loved helped them when nobody else would.

Both he and I began looking into the level of poverty in the area. There were too many families suffering the same plight. Some of them were too proud to ask for help and opted to endure their lot in silence. Michael was deeply distressed and decided to buy a three-bedroom house on the Fairlawn estate. He organised that two nuns from the Brigidine Order move in to alleviate some of the despair. By the time I came back to Finglas there were a number of trainee priests or deacons who regularly visited the parish and came to Michael for guidance. In fact, just as in every place Michael went, there were always people calling to the house for all kinds of reasons.

There was one of these men whom I did not like. When he visited the house he treated it like it was his and made me feel very uncomfortable. He didn't seem to like women much. One day, when Michael was out, this man was lying on the couch watching television. I was watching it from the chair by the fire. Ross came running into the room playing with some toy Michael had bought him when this guy suddenly lashed out and smacked him across the behind. Ross began to cry; apart from the odd slap I gave him, no one, including Michael, had ever touched him. I lifted Ross up in my arms and snapped: 'Is that how you are going to treat people when you become a priest?'

I left the room in disgust and I did not see him for the rest of the day. I didn't tell Michael about it. The next morning he arrived in the door with Ross and one of his pals. Ross had a new toy and ice-cream this guy had bought him. He was all charming and seemed to have undergone a complete transformation. But then he began making references to Michael and me. Then he made hints about Ross and who his father was. Somehow he had found out about us. I was petrified with fear.

Some years later I discovered that he found out while I was in America with Ross. It happened during a visit by my sister to see Michael at the presbytery. She had met this man there on a number of occasions and on this particular visit he was abusive towards her. They had a row and somehow she blurted out the details of my relationship with Michael in a bid to put manners on him. Instead, it gave him an idea to use it for his own wicked means Every time Michael wasn't around he would make the same snide remarks which left me in no doubt. He had complete control over me and he knew it. He even made the jibes in front of my friend Linda. He became abusive towards me and actually hit me a few times, once in front of her. She was furious and wanted to tell Michael and have something done about his behaviour. But I stopped her and told her of the risks of this guy exposing us.

Instead, I decided to put on an act for him, to pretend to like him so that he would keep his mouth shut. When Michael was busy he would ask him to take me shopping. He took me for a drink a few times and I met his family. One evening, in April, he suggested that he take me for a few drinks. Michael was going off playing poker and told me I should go, the break would do me good. He had no idea how much I hated being in this guy's company. I got a babysitter. We were only out an hour or so. He suggested I try Holsten Pils and I had two of them. I did not drink very often and it didn't take much to make me drunk. I had no idea just how strong this stuff was until I went out and the air hit me.

When he led me back to the house I said goodnight to the babysitter. I was a bit embarrassed because I was so tipsy. I said goodnight to him, looked in on Ross and went to my room. I was lying in the bed with my hands behind my head. The room was spinning around me and I vowed to myself that I would never have a drink again, I felt so rotten. Suddenly, I discovered that this guy was standing at the end of my bed. He had a wicked smirk on his face. He gave me a terrible shock because I thought I had heard him leaving and the door shutting behind him. I suddenly felt very scared.

'What are you doing here . . . what do you want?' I demanded. He put his fingers to his lips and said: 'Shush, you might wake Ross and we don't want that to happen.' He came over to the bed and caught my hands and pinned them behind my head with his left hand. I struggled against him, but with the weight of his body I couldn't move. With his other hand he pulled back the bedclothes and my nightdress and opened his trousers. I couldn't cry out or scream because Ross was in the room next to me and would be woken. In those frantic seconds I didn't want my child to come running in and witness what this bastard was doing to me. But I was screaming inside.

He forced himself into me . . . I can remember the pain, it was horrific. The memories of what my father had done to me came flooding through my mind. I went into a state of shock. I don't know how long it took before he had finished. It seemed like an eternity. He didn't look at me while he was doing it and his head was on my shoulder beside my ear. The sound of his grunts were sickening. Still panting, he pulled himself off me and lay back on the bed having satisfied his evil lust. I lay there staring at the ceiling. He was grinning like the cat who got the cream. 'I set out to get you and I got you, the Iron Lady.' I couldn't speak. I stared at him with disgust and hatred. He had planned this from the moment he found out about our secret. 'How could this man ever become a man of God?' I asked myself.

He kept on smirking and dropped another bombshell. 'Now I know what Father Cleary sees in you . . . you're a grand woman. I hope you won't be telling him anything about this, it would be a shame to upset him and Ross.' I froze with fear. I was too shocked and sickened by what had happened to reply. I got up off the bed and went to the bathroom. His words were like daggers being driven through my heart. I felt so used and abused. I ran myself a hot bath and scrubbed every inch of my body. I soaked for hours. I felt dirty, stupid and very frightened. How could I tell Michael what happened? If I did then he would surely throttle this would-be priest. I could see our world being exposed if this guy decided to press charges for assault against Michael or went to a newspaper or the bishop. Then I thought about going to the police and reporting the rape. But that, too, would bring unwanted notice on us.

Then there was the possibility that Michael could be blackmailed. It was too much to contemplate. Michael didn't deserve that.

I had practically no one to talk to and had no idea what to do next. It was some time before I even told Linda. When I got out of the bath he was gone. I tore the sheets off my bed and put on clean ones. No matter how much I had scrubbed myself in the bath I could still smell him. I felt sick. I couldn't sleep that night. I twisted and turned as my mind raced with all kinds of terrible thoughts. Some time later I heard Michael coming in from his poker game. I pretended to be fast asleep when he looked in on me. If he had come to me I would probably have broken down and told him everything. I made the only decision I could that night – to go on as if nothing had happened and somehow put this behind me. I saw the man who attacked me a few times after that but he didn't come near me. He even had the audacity to suggest that we both become friends. I told him I would kill him. After a while I didn't see him again around the parish.

My mind was so preoccupied with the hint of blackmail and exposure that I didn't have time to worry whether or not I was pregnant. Then the very thing I had given the least thought to happened. In May I found out that I was pregnant. I was completely devastated. I was also faced with the question as to whose child it could be. Michael and I still had a sexual relationship and I prayed that at least the child was his. I considered abortion but quickly put it out of my mind. I still remembered the suggestion made to Michael by a cleric friend of his when I was expecting Ross, that I have an abortion. I was disgusted by that, especially coming as it did from a holy man who publicly preached against it. I decided that I was having this baby and would deal with the problems as they occurred. I was wracked by confusion and guilt. It seemed that my life was dogged by one crisis after another.

I finally plucked up the courage and told Michael I was pregnant but nothing else. I would only find out who the father was when the child was born. Michael was understandably concerned. There was no way that we could have two children now and that broke my heart. But yet again we didn't spend much time discussing what to do. As before, the main concern was covering up. I suggested that I would have this child in America. He agreed with me and we checked out the price of having the baby in a hospital there. I also called Ivor Browne and went to meet him. I told him what happened. Ivor had always disapproved of the relationship between Michael and me on the grounds that it was potentially devastating for me. He advised me to tell Michael the whole story of what happened and then finally make a break. But I just couldn't take his advice, even though Ivor was right.

I called Phyl in Florida and told her I was pregnant. She was delighted for me, not knowing the full circumstances of the pregnancy. Michael and I decided that it would be best to leave Ross at home with him when I went away. In the meantime we had moved to a much more spacious presbytery which had two American-style apartments. We had two large bedrooms and two smaller rooms with walk-in closets and bathrooms en-suite. Linda agreed to move in and look after the two of them while I was gone. There wasn't the same risk of causing suspicion in Rivermount as there was in Ballyfermot. It was a more impersonal parish where the people just did their own thing. There wasn't the same level of integration between the clergy and the parishioners. I went to Florida in November when I could no longer hide the pregnancy. I was also violently sick most of the time. I told my mother and others that I was going to America because my friend was having a hysterectomy and I was going to look after her for a while.

I first attended the doctor when I went to Florida. He told me to go home and put my feet up. I was suffering with ulcers in my stomach and felt miserable. I was lonely for Ross and Michael and fearful for the future. By Christmas I couldn't wait for the birth. On 16 January 1985 Michael phoned me to

105

tell me that my father had died; he was 67. Despite everything that had happened I still loved him and had forgiven him. But I felt cheated that I had never had the opportunity to confront him and ask him why he had abused me as a child. Before that I had made my mind up that I would confront him after I came home from the States. But now it was too late.

Perhaps I had the opportunities in the past but just couldn't bring myself to ask. Michael had got on well with him and quite liked him. He often said that both my father and mother were good people in their own rights, but they were a disaster together. Nevertheless, there had been a strange bond between them which always brought them back to each other even though they were complete opposites. She looked after him right up to the time of his death. I think my father died a sad, lonely man with a lot of regrets. I didn't have much time to mourn. Two days after his death I went into labour.

The birth of my third child was an absolute nightmare. I went through 27 hours of the most harrowing labour. I went into the hospital at 9.30 a.m. on Thursday and finally gave birth to a baby daughter at 12.30 p.m. on Friday. I called her Felicia, which means happiness. I had decided to undergo a tubal ligation so that I would never again have children. I had the operation the next day. The following evening I felt very unwell. I called a nurse who gave me a sleeping pill. I didn't know that I was coming down with pneumonia, which was confirmed the following day. During the night I thrashed about in a fever and somehow managed to pull a ligament in my groin which added to the agony. To make matters even worse, as a result of the labour I was also suffering from haemorrhoids which had to be treated with heat lamps and ice. I was on intravenous antibiotics which caused severe diarrhoea. I was a complete physical and emotional mess.

Michael was called and told about my condition. He called every day to see how I was. I was frantic with worry and wanted to get home. In my delirium I was more scared that someone at home would find out that I had had a baby. I felt so bad I wanted to die. I would not have been able to look after the baby even if I had planned to take her home. Phyl had agreed to look after her for me while I worked out what to do back in Ireland. She was coming to Ireland during the summer anyway. After two weeks I was just about able to travel back to Dublin. Michael, Ross and my mother were there to meet me off the aeroplane. Michael helped me walk to the car and brought me home. I was hardly able to walk and got around with the aid of a chair. When we were alone I cried for a long time in his arms.

My recovery was slow. I still didn't know if Felicia was Michael's or not until I received photographs when she was three months old. There was no way she was like Ross or Michael Ivor. Phyl was due to come home with the baby in July. In early May I decided to break the news to Michael. One night, when we were alone, I told him everything. The first thing he said to me was: 'I had an idea when I heard it was a girl because all mine have been boys.' I had been afraid that he might doubt what happened to me – it is something that has happened to many women when they are raped. Michael was furious and cursed the guy who had done this to me. Later, I heard that the man concerned backed out of his ordination at the last moment. Michael told me later that there had been other problems and that he had talked to the bishop about it. I am not sure but I think Michael also went to see him before he made his decision. What matters is that I never saw him again.

Meanwhile, my mother and I were beginning to develop a closer relationship and she called around a lot to see the three of us. She adored Ross and had grown to like Michael, although she still regularly asked him to leave the Church and be a proper husband. She seemed happier than she had ever been. Following my father's death and the regrets I had about not sorting out our problems, I decided not to allow the same thing to happen with my mother. She was planning a visit to see Yvonne and Trish in the States. She celebrated her 63rd birthday with us. We had a cake and Michael, Ross and I sang

'Happy Birthday' for her. We got a video later on and were watching it when Ross came in upset. He sat beside his granny and told us that the other boys had told him there was no such thing as Santa Claus. She put her arm around him. 'They've probably been bad and their parents just told them that to get them to behave,' she told him, which cheered him up and he went back out to play. I smiled at her. Afterwards we had tea and Michael drove her home. She was in great spirits.

The following week Michael went around to bring her over to Finglas for a visit. He found her dead in a chair in the living-room. She had been there for a few days. When he phoned I was sitting at the desk filling in forms for the hospital insurance. I could tell that he was in shock. 'I have some bad news, Phyl. You had better get a taxi over here to your mother's . . . she is dead,' his voice was shaking. I threw the phone and the forms in the air and screamed. I was hysterical. Why were these things happening to me? What had I done to deserve so much pain? Just when I was getting to know and love my mother again she was taken away from me. Like my father, I didn't have the chance to clear the air between us totally. She had a dreadfully hard life, both my parents had. They had been slaves to circumstance. Despair had driven him to drink and her to prayer. It can't have been easy trying to rear seven starving children.

It was so unfair that she had not been allowed the time to go to the US to see some of her grandchildren for the first time. She had been so looking forward to that. Michael sent around another curate to comfort me. There was chaos in the next few days as we tried to contact all the family in England and America so that they could come home for the funeral. Michael buried my mother as he had done my father. That was very special to me. In the years since her death I have often felt guilty that maybe her worries about my relationship with Michael might have contributed to her death. A few weeks prior to her death she had again asked him to leave the priesthood and make a new life with us.

After the funeral I couldn't shake off the constant feeling of doom and gloom. Then, in July, Phyl arrived home with Felicia. I had my little girl for six wonderful weeks. She was such a healthy, happy little girl. I told Phyl about the circumstances of the baby's conception and she was upset that I hadn't told her before. But as the time came for Phyl's return to the States the subject of her future had to be addressed. Michael suggested fostering but Phyl blew her top. 'You can't do that, I've had her since she was born and it would not be fair on the child,' she said to both of us. Michael said that people would talk and point fingers. I could feel that I was losing control of the situation again.

I was confused and unhappy. I didn't want Felicia to become an object of curiosity and gossip. I wanted her to be happy. But I also had to consider Ross. If I moved away he would want to be with his father and neither of them would have the benefit of a stable family life with two parents. I felt that I had no right to cause this little angel any unhappiness, I had done enough of that to myself. So, I slowly came to the conclusion that it might be better to allow Phyl to adopt her. The adoption took a year to finalise and was done over the phone between here and the States.

It was a painful decision but, in the circumstances, the only one I felt I could make. My life has being punctuated with such decisions and heartaches. Afterwards I went into a black depression which lasted for about a month. Then one night I dreamt that all three of my children were back with me. My depression lifted and since then I have dreamed that it will happen.

At least I gave Felicia the gift of a stable home with two loving parents. Ross and I have travelled to see her and she has been here on holidays a number of times. Michael really loved her and she treated him like her uncle. During one of her holidays here, when she was three, we all went out to McDonalds. She looked across the table into my eyes for a few minutes and then asked out of the blue: 'Are you my

Mammy?' I looked up to heaven, swallowed hard and smiled back at her and Phyl. 'Sure you are such a lovely little girl everyone wants to be your mum.' I haven't seen Felicia for four years.

In that summer we got welcome news. Michael was to be promoted to the job of Diocesan Promoter of Missions and Retreats. We were to live in a private house at Mount Harold Terrace in Harolds Cross. At last we could live as a family without the difficulties of being attached to a parish. Michael was overjoyed and so was I. It was a lovely big old house with large rooms and four bedrooms. Michael had the attic converted as a play area for Ross. The day we moved in he held me in his arms and swung me around the kitchen. 'You see?' he said, 'God is on our side. We got this appointment because He approves. Now we can be a proper family.' That house became a warm, happy home. We were to suffer the same troubles any normal family suffers. For the first six years at least we were happy, although we did have parenting and relationships problems.

CHAPTER SEVEN

Problems at Home

IN HINDSIGHT, THE years after we moved to live in Harolds Cross was the first time we lived a relatively normal family life together. Normal, that is, behind closed doors when we were away from the smothering subterfuge and fear of exposure. By describing it as normal I am not trying to paint a surrealistic picture of suburban bliss. Far from it. We experienced the same troubles, heartache and disillusionment that an average family is likely to endure during a lifetime, except we suffered the additional stress of being forced to do so in secret. Upon reflection, it may appear contradictory, even sadistic, but the pain and the anxieties we encountered as a family unit during those few years still bring back happy memories. There was also a lot of love, fun and happiness in that house. When things were good they were really good. And when they were bad it was sheer hell.

In the five years following the move, Michael and I went through a series of crises which pushed our relationship to the limit of its endurance. The problems would have destroyed our relationship were it not for the sheer intensity of our love for one another. As parents we fought a lot over the way Ross was being reared and I felt that Michael was actively undermining me. But there were other problems before the issue of Ross's upbringing became a crisis. Apart from the external factors which, in 1992, would have a detrimental influence on events in our complicated secret world, the years preceding it were the most challenging period of our lives as a couple.

As a forty-year-old woman I went through the same problems as any mother and spouse. I found myself shackled to the kitchen sink, caring for two males who, in turn, appeared impervious to my needs. For all the years that I shared my life with Ross and Michael, I was the one who ensured that they had a comfortable home, clean clothes and the best of food to eat. I generally organised their lives for them. The two people I loved most in the complex situation I called my life, were simply taking me for granted. Although neither of them intended it that way, I felt justified in believing that I was being used. While I was at home sitting in the armchair of the front room watching the TV with only Bonnie the cat for company, Michael was off doing his thing. During the day he had a hectic schedule of stimulating diocesan work. At night he had his radio show on 98 FM and there were his poker games and racehorses. Ross had his life, too. He was either off somewhere with Michael or out with his friends. I was terribly lonely sometimes. Perhaps it was selfish of me, but I guess I was feeling sorry for myself.

There was the added strain of being seen as nothing more than the dedicated housekeeper to the outside world. Phyllis Hamilton was a scarlet woman with a son by an unknown father and a mysterious past which the average parish gossip found extremely titillating. I answered the phone and kept Michael's busy schedule in order. I was the one who made the tea for the constant stream of callers who came to Michael for help and advice. While he was the hero, sorting out everyone else's troubles, I was the unimportant, forgotten skivvy who, according to the outside world, lived off the support and charity of a great priest.

I was stultified; cluttered up. There were times I wanted to scream and tell the whole world our secret and then get on with our lives. I found the secrecy so hard to bear at times and I just wanted to be able to be acknowledged as Michael's wife. I needed to assert myself. I didn't want to be taken for granted any more. I was angry but not bitter or resentful. I didn't blame Michael. It was just an inevitable consequence of living such a double life. I simply wanted to establish my independence. That was when I met Tom.

In the early summer of 1990 I went for a holiday to Florida along with Ross to visit Felicia, who was now four. She had become such a beautiful little girl and it broke my heart that we had to return to Ireland without her. It was one of the things which plagued my mind that long, damp, dreary summer back in Dublin. It was an added strain imposed by the ludicrous celibacy laws of the Catholic Church which prevented a good, loving person like Michael Cleary to be a man as well as a priest. He loved Felicia and, if he hadn't been in the situation he was, would have been delighted to rear her even though she wasn't his. But the child we were rearing was now 13 years old and slowly beginning to go out of control, although neither of us would notice it for some time. Everything was getting on top of me. I was under a lot of stress. I was confused and agitated. I yearned to escape although I wasn't conscious of that at the time. Tom gave me that escape route.

I met him one night in July 1990 when I went to a pub on Wexford Street along with Roisin O'Shea, a niece-in-law of Michael's who had also become a very good friend. I had told her of our secret and so had Michael. She was very supportive to both of us. Roisin was meeting a friend of hers, Caroline, who reckoned this guy, Tom, might take a shine to her. ('Tom' was not his real name and I don't want to use it because I don't want to embarrass him . . . he was too nice for that.) I didn't go out very often at night, especially with Michael, and whenever I did it was mostly with friends. We were both nervous of going out for meals together because he was such a well known celebrity. We lived in fear of the tongue waggers.

There were about ten of us in the company in the pub. We sat around a big table drinking and having fun. When the gig was over, Tom came down to our table and joined us. He certainly stood out in the crowd and I could see why the girls were swooning over him. He had a dark complexion, was in his mid-30s, over six feet, with long curly hair. He had a lovely big smile and pearly white teeth.

Much to my amazement Tom took an interest in me and not in the other girls. I had practically no experience with men in my life. Apart from Michael, the few other encounters with men had been traumatic ordeals. Now here was this very charming gentle giant who seemed to have eyes for no one else except me. Through the years very few men had shown interest in me and this was the first man I felt comfortable with apart from Michael. I didn't feel sexually attracted to him at first, but I found myself wanting to be in Tom's company. He made me feel so special, so wanted. And he was different. I was extremely flattered that he liked me so much. I think it went to my head a bit.

After the pub we all went on to a late-night club. Tom stayed by my side for the rest of the night, laughing and cracking jokes. We danced a lot. I have always been a good dancer and he was impressed. He asked me to meet him the next day and I agreed. I was almost dizzy with excitement. Suddenly, I began to forget about all the problems which were brewing at home. I didn't feel like the forgotten housekeeper, mother and spouse. I was escaping from it momentarily. I knew that a relationship wasn't going to develop into anything but I wanted to enjoy every minute of this time. There was no sense of betraying Michael or doing anything behind his back. I wanted to be friends with Tom for the short time he would be around. I needed to indulge myself. At the end of the night he gave me a gentle kiss on the cheek and I got a taxi home with Roisin.

The next day Michael and I were in the kitchen. I was cleaning up as usual and he was sitting where he normally sat, reading the papers and keeping an eye on the racing on TV at the same time. I told him I had met this guy that I liked and I was going to see him that evening. He looked up from the sports page and attempted a smile. He seemed a little surprised and upset although he tried not to show it. I didn't want to upset him and explained that I would just like to meet Tom again because I enjoyed his company. I had always told Michael that if I met someone I liked then I would go out with him. In my mind there was never a threat to our relationship. But I was tired of the questions in people's faces which they never asked. They wondered about the unmarried mother who lived with the charismatic priest who never went out with other men. In my naïveté I also thought that going out with someone else would divert the attentions of the rumour-mongers from Michael.

He took a long drag on his cigarette, sucked in the smoke and looked into my eyes. 'Do you like this Tom fellah?' he asked quietly. I said that I did like him. Then Michael began asking how much did I like him and in what way. I said that I simply enjoyed his company and I wanted to see him again. I dried my hands, went over and sat on Michael's knee. We hugged for a few minutes. I told him that there was nothing to worry about. I rubbed his wispy hair and moved my face close to his. 'I just want to go out with somebody and feel what it's like to be normal for a change. I want to do the normal things that you can't do with me,' I said. When I left the house to go into town, he walked me to the front door. Before I opened it to step out of our secret world, Michael kissed me on the lips and held me for a few seconds. He wished me well and stood watching as I walked down the path, a cigarette hanging from the corner of his bushy beard and his hands stuffed into his pockets. Before I got into the waiting taxi, another caller was arriving for help and solace. In a way I felt sorry for him. I was getting a short break and he was back being the dedicated priest.

That evening was really enjoyable. Tom and I talked a lot but didn't discuss anything in depth. Tom was very gentle and

I felt that I was safe with him. I was with somebody that I knew wasn't going to abuse me. It was also a change to be out with someone without worrying about being recognised and talked about. He was fun to be with and we laughed a lot about silly things. We went to a picture and then had a few drinks. Afterwards he took me home in a taxi. During the trip he held my hand and kissed me. He made me feel wanted and I cradled my head on his shoulder.

I saw Tom regularly over the next few weeks. We went out to the cinema, for drinks, walks in the park and even took a trip to the zoo. Then one evening we made love in his apartment. It just happened spontaneously. I made love to Tom about three times in the few months that I knew him. One night he stayed with me in Mount Harold Terrace while Michael was away on a retreat. The sex wasn't anything special and I didn't feel an awful lot. I have never been a very sexual person. I always had hang-ups about it. The first man I ever made love to was Michael and I didn't enjoy it. In fact I could have lived my life without sex and still loved him just the same. But it was important to Michael and I wanted to show that I loved him. The relationship with Tom was frivolous. Through the years I had often wished that I could meet somebody I could love, even half as much as I loved Michael, and for that person to take me away. But Tom wasn't going to be the guy to do it. He was a wonderful man and, in a different life, we probably would have been made for each other.

Tom met Michael for the first time sometime in early August. It was one evening in the kitchen. I pitied Tom, with his big beaming smile, he had no idea of what he was standing in the middle of. Michael tried to smile as he extended his hand to shake Tom's. From that moment I saw a look in Michael's face that I didn't understand until much later. He hated Tom. He was furious and afraid at the same time. When we sat down to have tea I could see that Michael was frustrated in the same way that I had been all these years. I know he wanted to tell this bloke to sling his hook and leave his woman alone, but he couldn't. The need for secrecy restrained him. He wanted to express himself but couldn't.

Tom began calling regularly at the house. One night when he called the house was full of callers. There was a couple in the office, someone else in the kitchen and someone waiting in the front room to talk with Michael. It was such a regular thing. Michael would move from one room to the other, cracking jokes all the time trying to console and help in any way he could. He had a big heart and a deep love of people. He tried to help everyone who came to him, even those who exploited his immense generosity.

Tom suddenly arrived amid the shuffling of people and, because of the crowd, I stupidly suggested that Tom come up to my room and watch TV. We both lay on the bed talking and watching some programme. Nothing was going on between us. After a while, when the people had gone downstairs, Michael walked into the room as he usually did. He froze in the doorway. He hadn't seen Tom come into the house. Tom smiled and said 'Hi Father, how's it going?' Michael seemed uncomfortable and muttered: 'Oh, sorry, I didn't mean to interrupt. I was just saying goodnight. I'm off to the radio.' He looked at me and I could see the hurt in his eyes.

The expression on his face was one of disbelief that I had a man in my room. I was stupid and insensitive to have brought him up to the room like that. Later, when Tom had gone, Michael said very little except to ask me: 'What would Ross have thought if he had walked into your room tonight? I don't think that he would have been very pleased.' I said that I didn't think I was doing anything wrong. There were a load of people in the house and the only place I could take my visitor was to my room. I only realised later that during my short time with Tom, Michael was in absolute despair. He was jealous and angry at the same time. He felt threatened that this other man might take me away from him. He knew the high price I had paid during all those years of uncertainty and upheaval and reckoned that he did not have the right to put a stop to it.

Then he began interrogating me every time we were alone together. He bombarded me with questions like 'Where is this thing going between you and Tom?' and 'Where is it leading? Do you love him and has he asked you to go away with him?' I threw my hands up to heaven and said that the relationship was going nowhere and that was that, but he persisted. I didn't realise just how painful this whole episode was for him. I suppose I was being selfish, wrapped up in my little world without considering his feelings. And although I was not conscious of it, I think I was instinctively using the situation to assert myself, to demand more respect and love.

I didn't tell Michael that I had slept with Tom, although if he had asked I would have told him. It was an understood thing between us. I knew that he knew but he just didn't want it confirmed. Not saying things was a way of life in our bizarre little world. After all, Ross and Michael lived together as father and son for several years without the actual subject ever being discussed. He also had an idea of what it was all about, too. He had been unfaithful to me when I caught him in bed with one of the unmarried mothers who stayed in the house in Marino. But Tom was not my way of getting my own back. Although it hurt a lot, I had long forgiven him.

Michael was more experienced than me when it came to relationships. Although I was too innocent and naïve at the time to notice, when he first made love to me it was obviously not the first time he had been with a woman. There had been other times during our life together when I felt a strong suspicion that he had been with another woman. Michael was very warm, entertaining and charming and women liked him as a man. At every major function we ever went to there were always at least one or two women who fancied him. I particularly remember getting that feeling that he had slept with someone else, especially after he had been away on holiday a few times on his own. It was the way in which he reacted to me. I never had any proof, nor did I want it, in much the same way as he didn't want me to confirm that I had slept with Tom. By this stage we had been together over 20 years, by any standards a long time. A few suspicions, with the possibility that they were justified, is a drop in the ocean after two decades with someone you love.

During the Tom episode Michael and I continued to make love. We weren't prolific lovers. Sometimes we had sex one or more times a week and then we wouldn't have any for weeks. As we were lying in each other's arms he would continue to ask me questions about Tom. If at any stage he asked me to stop seeing Tom, I would have. In fact, deep down inside, I think I wanted him to be tough and assertive with me. But he didn't and he wasn't. One morning shortly after Michael found Tom in my room I awoke to find a folded-up piece of paper lying on the pillow where Michael had laid his head beside me the previous night. He had gone away on a retreat down the country much earlier that morning.

I unfolded it and found a poem which he had hand-written. He regularly left little love notes on my pillow, especially after nights when we slept together. But this poem was different. It was full of pain and fear and it almost broke my heart. It read:

You don't believe I love you, you don't believe I care,
I'm an egghead, I'm stupid, I'm a fool,
I'm a doormat others walk on, I'm just a handy tool
To be used by one and all while blindly unaware.

I'm a liar and a gigolo though no way debonair
I'm so thick you'd think I never went to school.
I'm dishevelled and untidy and smelly as a rat
With a scraggy beard, no teeth and just a crazy
    wisp of hair.

What have I got to offer? Why should anybody care?
For this pathetic relic of a man.
What claim have I to love, save from the Man above
As I sit here contemplating in my chair.

I'm a conman who has fooled his admirers everywhere
But where it matters I'm a failure and a wimp.
If character had legs I'd be walking with a limp.

I'm a burden I should not ask you to bear
Yet I have my simple dreams that I'd love
     someone to share.
Just a laugh, a joke, a smoke and a cup of tea
A companion, a love, a friend, who'd stick with
        me to the end.
And see through all my faults, a love that's
       sweet and rare.

When I read the poem my heart sank. I cried and cried for
hours. I saw the pain and the emotion in the words Michael
had put down on paper. Feelings that he could not articulate. I
hadn't thought much about how the relationship with Tom
was affecting him and suddenly I was reading it in black and
white. He had never told me how he felt. I never realised that
he was suffering so much. He didn't know that I would never
leave him and that Tom was just a brief episode in my life. A
brief respite from the drudgery and secrecy, nothing more. I
decided to end the relationship. Then, while I was cleaning his
room, I found another poem he had scribbled down on a note-
pad which convinced me of my decision. Writing these little
poems was his way of expressing his innermost feelings. It was
brutally honest.

Love requited or love denied
Are two experiences you cannot hide.

The joy of affection or the pain of rejection
Are too intense to be kept inside.

You may try to hide them and play a false part
But your face will reflect the true state of your heart.

Sometimes the truth dawns on you when it's too late
You are too busy to recognise true love or hate.

If it's hate you are better off not knowing it's there,
But unrecognised love can lead to despair.

So open your eyes before it's too late
For your lover may find that she just cannot wait.

If you take her for granted, she may look elsewhere
And you'll find very soon that you're left standing there.

It won't matter then what she sees in your face
In her heart someone else will have taken your place.

You can busy yourself with converting the city
And exist on the crumbs of her love turned to pity.

The absence of hate will be pure consolation
For the loss of her love will bring pure desolation.

You will love her alone for the rest of her life
But it's your fault, you never asked her

Would she be your wife.

The following evening Michael came back from his retreat. There was no one in the house. I put my arms around him and kissed him. We hugged for ages without saying anything. I cried and so did he.

'I didn't realise that I was hurting you . . . why didn't you talk to me, tell me how you felt . . . I was so stupid,' I said as I rested my head against his chest.

'I didn't think I had the right to tell you what to do. You have made more sacrifices for us than I have and you're entitled to your own life . . . I am a priest and I don't have the right,' Michael replied softly as he stroked my hair.

'I am going to drop Tom and get back to the way things were,' I said.

Michael cupped my head in his hands and looked me in the eyes. 'No, not if you don't want to . . . you don't have to.'

'It is what I want to do. I never wanted to hurt you, Michael, I love you too much for that,' I replied.

'I really love you, Phyl. Until this happened I didn't know just how much I loved you. I know I have taken a lot of things for granted and I am sorry, really, I'm sorry. I couldn't live without you or Ross.'

The relationship with Tom lasted for just over two months until September – not very long by any standards. And even though there was no major emotional attachment between us, breaking up with him was not going to be easy. I just couldn't turn around out of the blue and say, 'Listen, you will have to go because I have had a 22-year relationship with Father Michael Cleary, the man who ostensibly employs me as his housekeeper.' I decided just to gradually end things with him.

At the same time as I was seeing Tom, around September, I enrolled in a beauty school to study as a beauty therapist. It gave me an excuse to say to Tom that I just didn't have the time any more to see him. At first Michael disapproved of me doing it although he never said that I shouldn't. Before I got the poems, as a sign of his disapproval at my independence and my relationship with Tom, Michael would never offer to drop me at the school, even on mornings when it was pouring with rain. When Tom disappeared he could see that I had swapped Tom for the course. Michael left me at the school on Leeson Street every morning he could after that.

With Tom gone from my life Michael was much more free in himself and less cautious about people talking about us. We went out more often by ourselves for meals and he was much more affectionate and loving than he had ever been. Michael appeared to be a much happier man. He never mentioned Tom again.

CHAPTER EIGHT

Father Michael, the Parent

AS A PARENT Michael Cleary was a very loving and caring man who was totally devoted to his son. But in many ways he was also terribly irresponsible. He absolutely adored Ross but expressed that love by spoiling him beyond belief. From the time he was a toddler Michael ensured that he wanted for nothing. He never once raised his voice to Ross or reprimanded him, especially when he was going through the most recalcitrant stage of adolescence. In fact, Michael unwittingly contributed to Ross going off the rails for a time and not settling down at school. It was probably his way of compensating for the loss of our first son who was adopted. And he felt he had to make up for the fact that he could not publicly acknowledge to being Ross's dad. And Michael himself was an only boy who grew up with four sisters and spent most of his early life in boarding school.

So, while the brief, frivolous affair with Tom had ended by bringing us closer together as a couple, as parents our troubles were only beginning. After 1990 we had more and more rows about how Ross was being reared and what direction he was taking in life. I constantly worried that if Ross did not have control in this crucial stage of his development then he would fall into the wrong company and become a criminal, or worse.

But whenever I shared these fears with Michael he would laugh, saying that the child was just doing normal 'boyish' things and accused me of being over protective. The child could not do a thing wrong in our house. No matter what he did he was being a boy. He couldn't find it in his heart to be firm with him. And in the absence of a strong male figure in his life, Ross reckoned he could do what he wanted, just like any other kid his age.

They were very close to one another. Michael took him everywhere he wanted to go. He took Ross off to Cork to see Michael Jackson in concert, even though Michael couldn't stand his music. He sat there in the VIP stands reading a book by torchlight while Ross enjoyed the music. When Ross was happy and having a good time, so was Michael. Whenever he came home after being away for a few days or weeks on retreats or holidays, he couldn't wait for Ross to get up out of bed to see him. He planned one day to take Ross on holiday to Africa. Unfortunately, while he meant the best, Michael could just not say no to Ross. It got so bad that I felt he was unconsciously undermining me as a mother. He would say to me, 'When he is a child he is yours and when he is a young man he will be mine.' Michael was intensely proud of Ross. When he was a little boy and people would talk about the beautiful child, Michael would be so frustrated. 'It gets me in the gut because I can't acknowledge him the way you can,' he would often say.

I also had to take part of the blame for this crazy situation. Before I started the beauty therapists' course Ross was getting out of hand. But things deteriorated much further after I started. It was one of the biggest challenges of my life. I attended the beauty school every day and spent my nights studying. I decided to take the course because we were no longer living in a parish house where I was kept busy from morning until night. In Ballyfermot I worked closely with Michael in the parish and there was never a dull moment.

Since he got the new job I began thinking of doing

something else with my life. I wanted to have some sort of skill which I could use to go into business after Ross was reared and Michael had retired. Deep down I dreamt that when he reached 65 Michael would retire after a good career as a dedicated priest and would be able to live in peace well away from prying eyes and the Church – a place where we no longer had to worry about lies or secrecy. He had often asked me where I would like to live when he retired. He said he would be given a choice and it would be up to me. He suggested somewhere down in Wicklow where we could build a stable. He said he would buy me a foal, which he had often promised. I used to think after these conversations that maybe he would leave the priesthood and our secret would be a secret no more. Sometimes I only had my dreams to keep me going. It would be a pointless exercise speculating on whether any of them would have worked out. At least they were nice while they lasted.

My average day began before 6 a.m. and I would study until after 7 a.m. I would have a shower and then dress up like a beauty therapist with make-up and the whole works. Then I would call Ross and Michael and make them their breakfast. Michael often joked that he had a beautician waking him in the morning. 'It's just the sight to get you ready for the day,' he would say. I had to ensure that they both had clean clothes and helped get them both ready for their day. Sometimes it was like rearing two kids but I loved it. Then dinner had to be planned for the evening and shortly after 8 a.m. I headed off for school. After I had everything organised in the house at night, I studied until after midnight. It was hard going. In the beginning, partly because of my friendship with Tom, Michael wasn't very supportive and told close friends that he didn't think I would finish it. But when I completed the course in June 1991, with flying colours, he was very proud. Sometimes I regret that I ever did that course because I could have been home to keep a closer eye on Ross and there were times I considered packing it all in when he began messing around.

At night, while I was studying and Ross was supposed to be in bed, he would sneak out of his bedroom window and slide down the roof of the back extension to meet his friends. I was always nervous that he might slip and break his neck. Then his room was an appalling mess. There was acrylic paint all over the place, the bed and the carpets. One day he burned the curtain in his room. When I told Michael about it he smiled and said: 'Don't worry, that's the kind of thing a normal kid does.'

Then one day, to my horror, I discovered that Ross was smoking. Worse still, and what I wasn't to know until much later, was that he had been smoking for over a year with the full blessing of his father who even gave him the money to buy the damn things. I smoked a lot and Michael's most memorable characteristic was the cigarette dangling from the corner of his bushy beard. I didn't want Ross to ruin his health. When I told Michael about it he pretended not to know and said he would talk to the child. Michael talked to Ross all right. I found out much later that he advised his son that smoking was bad for him and a nasty habit. Then he grinned and gave him a further warning – not to get caught by his mother – as he offered him a fag.

That was the problem with Michael, he was a big boy himself and loved the villainy that young lads got up to. The same thing happened when I found out Ross was drinking. His reply was 'He might have a few drinks but that's all . . . there is no harm in it.' One night Ross rang Michael from somewhere in town. He had been drinking. One of his friends was so intoxicated that he was lying on the street unable to get up. I was upstairs in my room and heard the conversation on the phone. Michael did not get angry and just said to Ross to hold on and he would collect them immediately. I stormed down the stairs as he was going out of the door. I was so angry with him for being so easy on Ross. 'Do you want to get a call some night to go and pick Ross up out of the gutter or some hospital,' I shouted as the door shut. Then I had grounds to suspect that Ross and some of his mates were experimenting with soft drugs. They had smoked hash and this really concerned me. When I told Michael that I was afraid that Ross was at risk from getting into harder stuff, he refused to believe it or to even question his son about it. Thankfully, though, he didn't get into drugs.

At times I felt that our home was divided in two – with me on one side and Michael and Ross on the other. I often screamed at Ross and told him that as soon as he was old enough he was getting out into a bedsit of his own where he would have to learn how to look after himself. If Michael was around he would be highly offended. He would put his arm around Ross's shoulder and say: 'He will only go if he wants to and, anyway, Ross will never leave me, will you, Ross?' I would just have to give up in utter despair.

No matter how many times I argued with Michael he wouldn't change. Most of the arguments were one-way because he rarely argued back. He was a very peaceful man and had the most infuriating way of wriggling out of any situation I confronted him with. He would smile and sing 'Oh, don't be cross, my dear', which were the words in a Joseph Locke song, and I'd end up laughing with him. One night in the sitting-room we were having a row about Ross, or I was doing the shouting and Michael was barely answering me. I was infuriated with him that he wasn't listening, then the phone rang. I was in such a rage that I didn't give a damn who was on the line and whether they heard it or not. But Michael wasn't letting his guard down. So he picked up the phone in one hand and then literally sat on my head. There I was, suffocating under his backside, while he was laughing and joking to a relative on the phone. When the call ended and he let me up, all I could do was laugh and so did he. But our problems were by no means funny.

He was every kid's dream dad when it came to pocket money. When Ross was a kid of 13 or 14 his friends would get between five and ten pounds a week, if they were lucky.

Michael gave Ross a fiver a day and in most weeks topped it up to between £100 and £150. As a school-going teenager our son earned more money than a married man with children living on the dole! I couldn't count the number of times I chided Michael for giving Ross so much money. Whenever Ross was in trouble with me Michael would give him money to make up for it. But he would never tell me the truth. 'Ah, I only gave him a fiver,' he would shrug off my queries. Then Ross would stroll into the house after a day in town with a £50 jacket. Whenever he did talk to Ross about the way he was behaving he would hand over £20 or £30 and tell him to go and buy himself something but not to let on to me.

Whenever I grounded Ross, Michael would suggest taking him with him for his show on 98 FM. When they were gone he would drop Ross at a friend's house and collect him on the way home and I would never hear about it. Then Ross began to abscond from school, and when he was there he was getting into trouble a lot. During the period from 1991 to 1993 Ross was in and out of a total of five second-level schools. Michael sent him to the most exclusive private schools and paid the large fees. First there was St Mary's in Rathmines; then St Michael's on Aylesbury Road; St Mary's boarding school in Carlow; Synge Street and, finally, the Senior College in Rathmines. It was a nightmare. What made it worse was that whenever Ross got fed up with a school, Michael would use his contacts and shift him to another at the drop of a hat. Although I was never told at the time I now know that one of the reasons he was so unhappy was that other kids taunted him with rumours about Michael being his father.

On one occasion I discovered that Ross had not been at school for several days. It wasn't the first time I found out. In fact, there were several times he skipped off school for days and even weeks. I had chastised him until I was blue in the face about it and each time he said it wouldn't happen again. But it did. This afternoon I had had enough. I was furious. I was in the kitchen washing the dishes and Michael was sitting at the table reading the paper. When Ross came in I began scolding him. He walked off to his room and pretended not to hear me. I ran after him and accused him of smoking cannabis, saying that was the reason why he was not working at school. I told him that he was grounded and there would be no reprieve. When I went back to the kitchen I got little comfort from Michael, who always jumped to his defence. 'For Christ's sake, you can't ground him. He is an only child and he needs his friends' company. He needs to be with his peers, he's doing no harm. You can't wrap him up in cotton-wool for the rest of his life,' he stormed.

It was the same line I had heard over and over again. It was the last straw. I shrieked, 'Jesus Christ, do you ever listen to a damn word I say?' In a fit of desperation I took an ashtray out of the suds in the sink and flung it over his head. He put up his hands, which altered its direction, and it skinned his head on the way towards the wall. It bounced off the wall and smashed in a thousand tiny shards on the floor. I instantly regretted what I had done. It could have killed him. The ashtray had caused a small cut on his head and blood began to trickle from it. There was pandemonium. Michael got up and rushed upstairs to Ross, saying: 'Ross, Ross, look what your mother did.' Ross was terribly upset. A few minutes later he packed a bag and stormed out of the house. Michael stood there in the kitchen holding his head. 'If anything happens to Ross it will be on your head, he has to have some control in his life and you're not helping one bit,' I shouted at him.

There was silence after that and I cooled down. I felt sorry for Michael, standing there in front of me like a lost boy. I sat him down on a chair and examined the cut, which wasn't much more than a scratch. I got the first-aid kit and began cleaning it. I hugged him and he put his arm around me. He hardly spoke he was so upset. There were tears in his eyes.

'You know that I didn't mean to do that, it was an accident. If you hadn't put up your hands that wouldn't have happened,' I said.

'It'll be OK . . . I know you didn't mean it, but you're too hard on Ross. He's a good kid and he doesn't deserve it,' he assured me in a soft voice.

'We wouldn't be having these rows, Michael, if you took my side with Ross for a change and supported me when I'm trying to turn him into a decent human being.'

'I'll go and find Ross and bring him home, he'll be all right,' he said quietly.

We didn't say much then. We were still too upset and I put a band aid on his cut and we hugged each other for a long time.

Later, Michael got ready and headed off to do his radio show. I went upstairs to my room and found a note Ross had left for me on the bed. It broke my heart. It said something along the lines that I was the worst mother in the world and that if I ever hurt his 'Father', as we all called him, again he would leave for good. Michael up to that time had never told Ross that he was his dad. But both of them knew that the other knew. It was one of the strange aspects of our lives together. For all those years Michael lived as Ross's father but neither actually discussed it.

That night Michael made an appeal on his programme for Ross to call him. Ross called him and the next day Michael collected him from a friend's house and brought him home. When they came in Michael said that he had explained to Ross what had happened and that everything was going to be OK. All Michael wanted was peace. He always encouraged peace and there are a lot of people who can testify to that. Ross gave me a hug. There were a lot of tears. He said he wouldn't do it again. I said to him: 'I love you to bits, Ross, but I don't always like you. We have to sort out this mess for your sake because you have to get an education, because without one you will go nowhere.'

Unfortunately, despite the admonishments, Ross continued the same pattern in each school he went to. I was forever being called to meet school principals to discuss the situation.

Michael often came with me and both of us would talk to the teachers. They explained that Ross was not a bad child. He would just not turn up for classes, and when quizzed about it would only apologise and offer no explanation. I later discovered that there were many other times when Michael went to see them himself without my knowledge. When Michael sent him to his third school, as a boarder in Carlow, he only lasted a few months. He rang his dad and said he hated the place. Michael got in his car and took him home just like that. Then he got him a place in Synge Street in Dublin.

One afternoon someone left a message on the answering machine for Michael in Irish. When he came in he phoned the person back and began talking in Irish. When he finished I was very suspicious and asked him who he had been talking to. At first he wouldn't tell me. But I persisted and he told me it was a teacher from Synge Street. Michael had asked him to call him in Irish if there was a problem with Ross so that I wouldn't be worrying. Ross hadn't been in school for two weeks. He asked me not to say anything to Ross, that he would deal with the problem himself. But I was nearing the end of my tether. Now Ross was telling me blatant lies. Each morning he had gone off to school and returned in the evening telling me about the day he had had. When Ross came in I insisted on bringing it up. The three of us sat around the table and Michael, for once, backed me up.

Michael would never raise his voice or lose his patience with Ross. He said to him: 'Ross, if you don't pull up your socks at this school, you are going to be kicked out. If you would only settle into a school and get your Leaving Cert you can do what you like. You can go to the best college: the money is there to pay for it.' But again Ross promised to do better and Michael accepted it. Then the same thing happened all over again. And when it did, Michael was there to cushion the blows. On one occasion I was so exasperated that I decided I needed a break and headed off to London for a week to visit my sister and leave the two boys at home on their own.

Michael thought that I had run off with Tom and he went to see some of my friends to ask them if this was the case. Nothing could have been further from my mind. I was just trying to show both Ross and Michael that I had had enough, Michael again agreed to help sort out the mess.

But eventually, when the situation didn't change, Michael began to accept that I was right. One day I got a call from the school saying that Ross had not been in class for two weeks. I was in despair. At the same time there were two young English TV producers staying in the house. They were making a documentary with Michael. I was on a knife-edge. I was trying to keep up the front to these people and at the same time trying to address the problem with Michael.

That afternoon, when I mentioned it to him, he decided to go to bed for a nap and left me standing in the kitchen with these two strangers. I ran upstairs after him. I was very upset and began crying. I burst into Michael's room and said to him, 'You bastard'. I grabbed my coat and ran out of the door. I went into town. I was feeling very shaky. I went to see a movie, appropriately called, *Shattered*. Afterwards, I walked around for a while and took a bus home. As usual the place was full of callers and Ross was out somewhere with his pals. There was Michael holding court, talking to them and helping sort out their individual problems while at the same time, I felt, ignoring the most important one of all, his own son.

I ran upstairs and lay crying on my bed. So many things were going through my head. I felt helpless, desperate. Ross was just running wild and I was powerless to do anything about it. And if Michael would only be the parent he should be, we could get Ross back on the tracks again. I was also beginning to doubt myself as a parent. Maybe I was the one who was wrong. Maybe I should have heeded the advice from Michael and his friend, Eamonn Casey, and had Ross adopted like the other two children. My mind was in a spin.

When the callers had left, Michael came up to the bedroom. He sat on the edge of the bed beside me. I was still crying. He put his arms around me. 'You don't know how much I love you and Ross . . . you just don't know,' he whispered.

'But you can't love him that way, you can't keep giving him money and letting him off with everything he does, that's not loving him,' I replied.

'I don't know how else to do it. I know there are problems but he is a good boy and he is just a bit mixed up.'

'Well, you will have to start appreciating the fact that my instincts are not wrong.'

We never really resolved our differences as parents after that and the problems with Ross continued, only I learned to cope with the situation better. But events outside our secret world were to overtake our problems, making them seem trivial by comparison. Ominously, dark storm clouds were gathering in the distance. It would be a storm like no other which would threaten to destroy our world.

CHAPTER NINE

The Casey Affair

IN EVERYONE'S LIFE there is a single event, a moment when their whole world suddenly comes crashing down. A sudden and dramatic change which has a profound influence on a life and remains etched in the consciousness until the end of that life. For me that day was Thursday, 7 May 1992. The day the whole country awoke to hear the astonishing news that Bishop Eamonn Casey had fathered a son.

In the days before the news broke I couldn't sleep properly and I was very restless. I couldn't put a finger on what it was that was making me so uneasy. Deep down something was worrying me. Whenever I felt that way I knew something was going to happen or some problem would arise. Michael went to Spain on the previous Saturday, 2 May, with a group of friends. He went there every year for a week of golf. Before he left I packed his bags for him and we kissed and hugged each other before he left. The night before we had made love together in my room. Ross was settling down a bit and we were relatively happy. He was full of the joys of life. He always looked forward to that trip.

On Wednesday night I went to bed feeling really tired but I was unable to sleep. Just before I went to bed I moved the phone on the table beside my chair in the living-room. A small piece of paper was sticking out underneath. It was the prayer of St Francis of Assisi which Eamonn Casey had given to me some years earlier after one of his visits. He had signed it on the end. I had a habit of putting pieces of paper like that under the phone. It was a strange coincidence.

I tossed and turned until around 5 a.m. I got up, put on my dressing-gown and went downstairs. I did bits and pieces around the kitchen and sorted some laundry. Then sometime between six and seven I heard the *Irish Independent* being dropped through the letterbox. We had it delivered to the house every morning. I thought to myself, 'Good, I can read the paper and have a cup of tea and I might be able to go back to bed.' I walked up from the kitchen into the front hall. The paper was lying there on the mat, folded with the top half facing me. As I went up the two steps which lead into the front hall I could see the big black letters but couldn't make them out.

I bent down and as I picked it up I froze. I don't remember the headline but there it was . . . Eamonn Casey had a child. I couldn't read the words. I was in a state of shock. It was as if I had been struck by a bolt of lightning. My mouth was dry. I couldn't swallow. A cold shiver of sheer terror ran down my spine. I turned and limped back to the kitchen holding the paper out in front of me just as I had picked it up. I put it on the table and sat down staring at the front page. I wasn't able to read it. My past and future flashed before me at the same time. I could see our secret life as a family, the secret we had managed to keep for all these years, suddenly destroyed. I could see Michael, Ross and myself on the front page, exposed like criminals. My mind was racing faster than I could think straight.

When I got a grip on myself I read the story. It was the first time I saw the name, 'Annie Murphy', the American divorcee Eamonn had a son with. Then it dawned on me: 'Jesus, he has a son not much older than Ross'. My mind was a muddle of different emotions. I was confused. There were so many questions buzzing around my brain. I thought: 'All the time Michael and I had spent with Eamonn discussing our relationship he also had a secret.' Then I wondered if Michael knew about it. I wanted to call him in Spain. My hands were sweating and shaking uncontrollably as I went to the phone. I decided not to call him just yet. Then I tried to dial Eamonn's number in Galway but it was busy all the time.

I sat there in silence at the kitchen table, staring into space. Sometime before 9 a.m. the phone made me jump in my seat. It rang a few times before I picked it up. 'Hello, Phyl! Is Michael there?' Eamonn Casey's voice did not have its usual jolly tone. It was full of panic. He was breathing fast and sounded like he was in a hurry. I didn't know what to say to him in those few seconds.

'Eamonn, I am so sorry,' I heard myself say. 'He is away golfing.'

'I am rushing . . . I am going away. Tell Michael I won't be back for a long time. Thank him very much for everything he has done for me. I must go, goodbye Phyl.'

His voice disappeared behind the monotonous tone of the phone line. I was overwhelmed with a feeling of pity for Eamonn. I hated this woman, Annie Murphy. 'The bitch,' I thought angrily, 'that fucking bitch is going to turn all our lives into a nightmare. Why didn't she keep her mouth shut and leave us in peace.' Later, I realised that I was not in a position to judge Annie Murphy. In my despair I believed that Michael and I would be next in the firing line of, as I saw it, a hungry, heartless media, hell bent on destroying people's lives. I was falling apart at the seams. I was screaming inside, thinking how hurt everyone would be if they found out about us. It would devastate Michael and Ross. What would we do? Where would we hide? I wanted to wrap my arms around the two of them and protect them from this nightmare. In those few hours the whole world had become my enemy.

When I had composed myself sufficiently, I went up and woke Ross around 10 a.m.. As he sat up in the bed and rubbed the sleep out of his eyes he read the anxiety in my face. 'Is Father all right, has there been an accident?' he asked nervously. I told him about the paper and the call from Eamonn. Even though he had lived with our secret for most of his young life it was a lot for an already mixed-up 15-year-old to take in all at once. It took a long time for the enormity of the situation to impact on him. The story was all over the radio and on Sky News. I didn't want to call Michael but I knew that he would know what happened.

The following two days were a blur. The phone remained remarkably quiet. There were no journalists calling yet. It was like they knew he wasn't home. I couldn't sleep or eat. I smoked cigarettes and waited for Michael to walk in the door. I dug out loads of poems, cards and letters in which Michael had expressed his love for me and burned them. I also emptied a drawer which contained what Michael used to refer to as 'fun clothes'; these were items of lingerie he would buy for me while he was abroad or in England. In my delirious panic I felt that someone might break in and find them. The minutes and the hours couldn't go fast enough. On Saturday morning I was in the kitchen with Ross.

I heard the key in the door. My heart missed a beat. Michael walked into the hall with a golf bag in one hand and a case in the other. He was wearing a maroon sweater over a summer shirt and slacks. Whenever he came home from a trip he would have a big beaming smile, delighted to be home. There was no smile. His face was a little tanned but I could see that he was ashen underneath. We made eye contact the second he walked in. I knew he had heard the news.

Michael was a changed person. It was a devastated, broken man who stood before us. He dropped his bags and came into the kitchen. He stretched out his long arms and embraced the two of us. We all hugged like there was no tomorrow. There were tears, plenty of tears. Michael held us tightly. 'We are a family and we will get through this thing together. No one will split us up.' Then he looked at Ross. 'Ross, you are my son, I am very proud of that and I love you.' It was the first time that he had ever said those words to Ross. He nodded to his father, tears welling up in his eyes. Then he looked down at me. 'And you are no Annie Murphy.' I sobbed on his shoulder. There were few other words spoken. The sense of fear was palpable. It was like the three of us were under siege.

Then the phone started hopping. It was as if the reporters were sitting outside and knew the precise moment to call. Every paper in Ireland and England must have called that day. I just wanted to rip the phone out of the wall and silence the lot of them. Other reporters were knocking at the door. He hated the lot of them. Michael had no choice but to face the public. He was a master performer. For 24 years he had been able to live a double life but this was tough on him. He was shaking in his shoes.

We had little time to talk. A former parishioner of Michael's called at the house. It was the last thing I needed. I began pretending that nothing was wrong and tried to put up the housekeeper front. I was ready to explode in a flood of tears. Then Michael said reassuringly, 'She knows.' I began to cry. The woman was one of the people Michael confided our secret in. She was very supportive. (Unfortunately, following Michael's death, when I was still hiding from the world, this same woman was one of the people who denied us. She really hurt Ross when she told him that he was not Michael's son and suggested that I was a mad woman!)

Michael had little time to think in those first few weeks. I could see that he was deeply hurt by the realisation that his friend, Eamonn Casey, had not trusted him enough to tell him his problem. He felt betrayed. Michael wanted us all to ride out the storm, brazen it and behave like nothing had happened. He said that if our secret was revealed then he would come up smelling of roses because he had looked after his responsibilities and never denied Ross. And he said that if they (the media) got evidence about Ross he would admit it. 'Eamonn Casey is the horror story, but we are the love story and no one can condemn us for that,' I remember saying to him.

But he lived in dread of that question. I don't believe that Michael would have been able to deny his son to the world. But I know that he was terrified of being exposed because of what his own Church would do to him and not how the public would react. He told one of his relations who knew our story, that the Church would pack him off to South America the same as they did to Casey. Michael was a born and bred Dubliner and could not live anywhere else in the world except with his own people. He had spent practically all of his career among the people he loved. I don't think he would have been happy in any parish outside Dublin. Although he didn't tell me at the time, being forced to leave the country would have probably destroyed him.

Every time he answered the phone to a reporter in those first days he was swallowing dry. One day, when we were alone together, he said that he was a little afraid that the woman I found him in bed with back in 1971 might come forward. Then three days later, 12 May, Michael was called to a press conference to face the people he disliked most, the press. But this time it was a happy occasion, Michael received the Performing Artists' Trust Society award for his charitable work as the singing priest. He was deeply honoured. But at the press conference he was not his usual cheerful, lighthearted self. He looked nervous and downcast. He thanked PATS for their award with the comment: 'It is nice at a time when people in my world are feeling very, very low.'

Michael suggested that we prepare for the worst. We both talked to a close friend of ours who had known of our relationship for a long time. He advised us to have what he called a 'doomsday' plan, prepared in case we, too, came into the media spotlight. Our passports were out of date but Michael had them renewed for Ross and me within five days. The plan was that in the worst case scenario the three of us would flee the country. I told Michael that Ross and I would move out to a flat and live well away from Harolds Cross in a bid to deflect any possible speculation about us. But Michael was totally against that. He didn't want to be without his son. Upon reflection I also have to look at the possibility that he was making sure I was around so that he knew where I was and could control me.

Ross was very brave throughout all this. He was quiet and reassuring to both myself and his father. He still went out with his friends although he was a lot more cautious. We were both scared for him. Upon reflection, it was probably a lot harder on him than either myself or Michael could have imagined. He was going through the toughest stage of puberty and no doubt he was taunted plenty about the rumours by other kids. As part of our plan of action Michael said we should be careful at all times, especially answering the door or the phone, in case we were caught on the hop.

Meanwhile he continued to face the media and the world pretending that nothing was wrong. He defended his friend at every opportunity, even though he felt totally let down by him. The day that he made the remark on a radio programme that at least Eamonn hadn't asked Annie Murphy to have an abortion I was sitting with him in the kitchen. He caused outrage by those words but Michael didn't mean them. I was hurt for him when he was criticised so severely. I wanted to protect him, the politically correct critics had no idea what a good man he was. He was in turmoil, saying things without thinking. The Catholic hierarchy, who have a habit of hiding behind people like Michael, should have been answering those questions.

Then a week or so later an English reporter came to the door. Michael answered it. He accused Michael of being the father of another woman's daughter. The woman concerned had been a friend of Michael's but never had a relationship with him. He almost threw the reporter out of the house in a fit of rage and flatly denied the rumour to anyone who asked. He said that he was prepared to take blood tests to prove that he hadn't fathered the child. It was this denial by Michael which was used by some of his friends in their rush to deny that Ross was his son. In a way the rumour helped divert attention away from the real story.

As the weeks dragged on Michael appeared to be a little more relaxed. He kept putting pressure on me to go out with him as we had done before. He felt that we had done nothing wrong. 'We'll go out to the Dropping Well for lunch, the same as we have always done. We will go out that door, get in the car and drive off the same as ever. Let them do what they like,' he coaxed me over and over. But I was terrified and wouldn't go out the front door. After May 1992 I never left Mount Harold Terrace by the front door again. 'Nobody, but nobody, is going to catch me with you and get a photograph. What will you do if they splash it all over the bloody papers?' I would reply. Whenever I did go out it was through the back door.

From the time our relationship began I had trouble living a double life, but the lie was the price I had to pay to stay with the man I loved. I could never tell a lie, that's why I kept myself isolated from an awful lot of people through the years. If I got very friendly with someone I would feel compelled to tell that person our secret. Michael didn't mind because he trusted my judgment of people. He could relax then in the company of people who knew the situation. Every time I switched on the TV or radio, or picked up a paper, they were discussing Casey.

I felt so awful that I couldn't even look Ross's friends in the face. I spent a lot of time in my room. In hindsight, I have to confess that I wasn't much support to Michael or Ross. Every day Michael tried to get me to go out but I couldn't. He was always hugging me and reassuring me, but it did no good. Neither of us could make love during that time either. The situation was just too intense for that. I stopped eating and I couldn't sleep at night. I was getting panic attacks and a friend of Michael's, Peg O'Connell, a doctor who was also Ross's godmother, gave me some valium but they were of no benefit.

I had a phobia about taking pills. Things got so bad that the very mention of Casey sent me running to the bathroom. My whole body was pulverised with an uncontrollable fear. For weeks I locked myself in my room refusing to come out for anyone. The whole thing had driven me to the point of a nervous breakdown.

At the end of July Michael was very concerned about me. He called Ivor Browne and he came to see me at the house. Ivor was one of the few people who knew everything about our relationship from the beginning and he knew what I was going through. He recommended that I get out of the house for a few weeks for a rest. We had to ensure it was somewhere discreet, where no one would know that it was Michael Cleary's housekeeper and then put two and two together. Ivor arranged for me to go into St Vincent's, a psychiatric hospital in Fairview, for sleep and rest. Roisin O'Shea and her husband, Don, took me there on Saturday, 25 July.

Although there was a pleasant atmosphere about the place it brought back horrible memories of when I was an inmate in St Brendan's. I still couldn't sleep, even though they had me on heavy medication. On the first evening a nurse began going through my luggage looking for valium because I couldn't sleep. She kept asking me if I had any hidden on me. I began to scream and shout at her. When she had gone I got dressed and headed for the door. To my utter dismay it was locked. I began reliving the horrors of my early experiences in psychiatric care and I went into a panic.

I decided to make the most of this 'rest period'. I just wanted to get home to Michael and Ross. A few days later I asked to see them and was told that only one person could visit. This really threw me into shock and panic. The next day I was coming from the bathroom when I saw Michael down the corridor talking with a nurse. My heart jumped and I went into my room and brushed my hair for his visit. Then I discovered that he had been advised that it would be unhelpful for me. I had been through this unbelievable nightmare outside and after all that here I was isolated and alone. At that moment I decided that I wanted to get out of that place.

I slept in my jeans with a t-shirt under my nightdress. I went into the bathroom and tried to burn the ropes on the windows so I could get out. It didn't work. The ropes were sturdy and the lighter got too hot to hold. Then on the following Friday, 31 July, a cheerful cleaning lady came into the room and said, 'It's a lovely day, why don't you go out in the garden?' I went out into the gardens in my dressing-gown. I walked slowly at first and then speeded up. I went behind some bushes, dropped the dressing-gown, tucked the nightdress into my jeans and took off.

When I got out of the gate I didn't know which way to turn. I hailed a taxi. At first I was going to go straight home but figured that it might be dangerous, so I was dropped in town. I was paranoid and terrified. I went into Dunnes and bought a top which was on sale for £2.99. Then I had my hair done just to pass the time. Then I went into Clearys to buy a bra. I hadn't enough money to buy one, so I took a bunch and went in to try them on. I kept one on and left the rest and walked out, praying that I would not be caught. Eventually I phoned the house. Michael answered, he was frantic. I refused to tell him where I was until he promised not to tell the hospital. He collected me outside Wynn's Hotel. He held my hand so tight all the way home in the car. He told me I looked beautiful. We got into the house and he broke down and cried.

'God, Phyl, I was so afraid . . . I wanted to see you but I was advised against it,' he hugged me tightly to his chest.

'I ran away because I was afraid and I wanted you to see that I was all right,' I told him.

We hugged for the longest time. There were a few calls from the hospital but Michael said I wasn't there. Later on he went to the radio and I sat in the armchair attempting to relax.

In the months that followed the situation relaxed a little although I didn't, simply because I couldn't. No matter how much reassurance, support and love I got from Michael and Ross, I was on edge all the time. From then on normal life in our house was nothing more than putting on a brave front. There was a constant state of alert, waiting for that fateful knock on the door or phone call which would pull back the curtains on our secret world. Every morning Michael got up, listened to the radio and scanned the papers as if he was checking to see the coast was clear before he faced the world. The tension returned every time the Casey affair came up in the media. And that was a lot for the rest of 1992. Although he tried hard not to show it I know he lived in constant dread.

One of the stories which did upset Michael most was news that Eamonn had sneaked back into the country for a secret visit with close family and friends. It added insult to injury for him. It crushed Michael when he did not hear from the friend he had been so loyal to. He felt betrayed. One day, after he read that Casey was back in the country, Michael didn't leave the house. Every time the phone rang he answered it in the hope that it was Eamonn. Whenever Michael enquired about Eamonn's phone number in Central America, no one seemed to have it. It made him feel like he wasn't trusted although he still had great sympathy for his old friend.

As the months went past Michael continued to put pressure on me to resume our lives the way they had been. He thought that the heat was off but in my mind I thought that it was never going to be off. Judging by the events which followed his death I was proved correct. We had a lot of rows about it. 'You have to go out, you must,' he would say. I would reply, 'No, just stop. Let this thing take its course with me.' I was so terrified that there might be a nosey journalist around a corner or a photographer trying to catch us together. I just wanted some kind of peace and quiet. I didn't want to go anywhere or talk with anyone except the handful of close, trusted friends I had. I stopped going to Mass even though I loved it and still do. He wanted others to see me 'do the right thing'.

In January 1993, I just couldn't take it any more, although I know Michael was doing what he thought was best for us in the situation. One night I had a vivid dream about being a little girl again. Someone told me that I was the image of my mother. It blew my mind. I had always hated being compared to my mother. It was the reason I believe that my father abused me as a child. I blamed her for everything that happened in my earlier life; for the orphanages and the effect they had on me. I blamed her for the circumstances which led to my meeting Michael and, ultimately, for the pain we were now suffering. When I woke up I was in a daze. All I can remember is saying to myself that I will never look like my mother again.

I got up and went down to the kitchen. I reached into the cutlery drawer and took out a knife. I went back up to the room and sat on the bed with the knife in my hand. I cut my right cheek to pieces with it. Then I just sat there with blood all over my clothes and the bed. When Michael got up he came into the room to wake me. He was horrified at what I had done. He raced over to me and held me in his arms. 'Oh, why, why, why did you do it?' he asked in a hoarse voice.

I said: 'I don't want to be a hypocrite anymore. I don't want to be exposed to the whole world as a fraud. Now I won't have to go out like you keep asking me.'

'I never wanted to force you to go out,' he gasped.

'I can't go out now with my face like this,' I replied.

From that moment Michael never tried to force me to go outside. I saw the realisation on his face of the harm the pretence was doing to me. Michael got a towel from the bathroom and began to clean up the wound as best he could. He said that it needed stitches and wanted to take me to a doctor or hospital. I wouldn't let him. If I walked into a hospital or a doctor, what would people think, I told him. I still don't regret what I did. It was as far as I was prepared to go not to be a hypocrite. Some people would say that I was psychologically unbalanced. They can say what they like. There were times I wished I was. That I could be taken away and have all this truth taken out of my head. After that, Michael went to see Ivor and brought him back to the house. I told Ivor the same thing I had told Michael. Although what I did was drastic and disturbing, our lives did get back to some kind of normality amid so much chaos.

Michael was never more loving after that. He finally understood what a toll our bizarre life was having on me. I stayed inside most of the time. I read and studied a lot and did what I wanted to do most, love and care for Michael and Ross as a mother and wife, away from the wink and elbow language of the outside world. But life would never be the same again for us after the Casey affair. It would have tragic consequences for us.

CHAPTER TEN

The Final Kiss

IN THE MONTHS following the incident when I slashed my face things began to calm down somewhat in our panicked household. When I cut myself I was expressing my inner turmoil and fears. Being able to stay away from the outside world without any pressure from Michael, I was much happier. But now I worried a lot about him, he internalised most of the anxiety and worries created by the Casey affair. Although we were extremely close and he was so loving to me and Ross, he was a changed man.

I knew that in particular he dwelt a lot on the secret side of his life and deep down inside wanted an end to the subterfuge. He desperately wanted to be able to live as a priest as well as a father and husband. When he actually told Ross he was his dad, it made him much happier, even though it was in an atmosphere of panic and fear. He grew even closer to Ross. But it worried him that members of his immediate family did not know. They had always been very warm and welcoming to Ross and me. We regularly visited their homes with Michael spending every Christmas there. They would buy presents for us and generally treated us very well. It seemed to me as if it was taken for granted that we were like a family unit; perhaps deep down that is what we wanted to believe. But I felt bad for

Michael that, apart from his niece, Roisin, he had not confided in any other members of his family. One day I decided to do something about that.

On 28 March 1993, I picked up the phone and called a relative of Michael's and told her about Ross. She seemed taken aback and arranged to come around to the house to discuss the matter the following morning. I felt it was time that it was all out in the open with the people who mattered. We had enough on our plate to worry about the media and the rest of the world outside. When I told Michael what I had done he was annoyed for a while and then seemed relieved that he could finally reveal his secret to a close relative. I said: 'All of my family have known about us for a long time, all of them, and I can talk to them about us and you are relaxed with them. But you have no one belonging to you, apart from Roisin, who you can share the truth with.' That night I was nervous and could barely sleep: neither could Michael. The following morning the relative arrived. I was in the kitchen with Michael. Ross was upstairs. I had known this woman for a long time and had been friendly with her. She was defensive and had changed towards me.

Michael stood there and told her that what I told her was true. He seemed a little shaky, his voice was soft and gentle. I was standing near him but there was no holding hands as a sign of solidarity. The atmosphere was decidedly tense. The woman could not accept any part of the story. In hindsight, I can understand that. It was shocking news for her. She had known Michael all her life and loved and respected him as a priest. Like the rest of his family she was very proud of his achievements. Like the rest of us, she was also afraid of what something like this would do to the family if it became public knowledge. Then she turned to me and suggested that because I had been sexually abused as a child, I was sexually more experienced than Michael. It seemed to her that I had an advantage over him. I couldn't believe what I was hearing. When I met Michael I was a 17 year-old virgin, still suffering the trauma of a nightmare childhood, and he was 34 years old. When I had our first child I was 20 and Michael told me that I was too young and immature to have a child. Michael was visibly upset by what he was hearing and his face went white. I burst into tears.

Then she brought up the subject of Felicia and talked about the man who had raped me. I felt that I was being blamed in some way for having this child. That I had been having an affair with this man. I regained my composure and asked her why she thought the person in question had refused to allow my complaints to be investigated. Why had he walked out and left the priesthood just months before he was ordained? I did not want to fall out with this woman. She was a kind, good-living woman and I had a lot of respect for her. I just wanted her to understand the situation.

Ross had been sitting on the stairs listening to the argument about him. Michael went up and brought him down to the kitchen. He stood there with his arm around Ross and told the relative: 'Ross *is* my son and he has not done anything wrong here.' Ross was scared out of his mind by all this commotion. She calmed down after a while and was very nice to Ross. She accepted that he had done nothing wrong. After a few cups of tea she left the house. I said I was sorry for upsetting her and we seemed to be friends again.

In May we got another jolt. This time we learned that Roisin O'Shea had contacted the Archbishop's office anonymously and informed his secretary of the truth of our relationship. She did it with the best will in the world, although it was misguided at the time and I didn't agree with it. She was frustrated and worried about the effect the Casey affair had had on Michael and me. She also wanted to ensure it was known in case anything happened to him. When I told him what she had done he was silent and stared into space. I know he was deeply annoyed but tried not to show it. He later visited Roisin and they had words about it. But in the meantime we put it behind us because the call had been

anonymous and we knew nothing would come of it at that
stage.

In the year since the revelations about Eamonn Casey,
Michael's health visibly deteriorated. He was very hoarse and
coughed a lot. I was always at him to go to a doctor and have
it checked out. I remembered the warning from the doctors 18
years earlier that the cancer could recur. I often worried about
that. Two years earlier a doctor had given him a letter to go for
an x-ray at the hospital but he hadn't bothered. Michael was a
big strong man but at the same time didn't want to know if
something was wrong. At night his coughing would wake the
dead. 'For crying out loud,' I used to say to him, 'will you do
something about getting that cough checked out.'

Then one night in July, I had a disturbingly vivid dream.
Everyone we knew was in the house. Someone came up to me
and said I'd better go to Michael because he needed me. I
rushed to the sitting-room and stopped in my tracks. I could
see Michael falling back on the side of the couch with his arms
outstretched. He wasn't able to talk but I sensed him trying to
say: 'If you don't do something about this no one will.' I woke
up in a cold sweat. I could hear him in his room coughing in
his sleep. I got out of bed and went down to the kitchen and
sat there smoking cigarettes and drinking cups of tea until
around 8.30 a.m. when I could call a doctor. I phoned his
friend, Peg O'Connell, and impressed upon her the urgency of
getting Michael an appointment in St Luke's as soon as
possible. Later that day Peg rang Michael and told him she had
made an appointment for him to see his doctor. At first he was
reluctant. 'I think I know who is behind this,' he said down the
phone turning to look at me.

The next day we left him in the hospital to undergo a day
of tests. That evening Roisin O'Shea and her husband Don
collected Michael. We waited for ages and finally he came
through the doors with a nurse and a doctor. He appeared
groggy but all the facial expressions and negative vibes
coming from everyone said so much more than words. I was

worried but took solace from the dream. I figured that it was a warning and so eventually everything would be all right, that whatever was wrong had been caught in time for treatment. A short time later we got a call from the hospital saying that the tests had been 'inconclusive' and Michael would have to go in for further tests, scans and biopsies.

A date was set for him to go into St Vincent's private hospital on Sunday 29 August – exactly seven years from the day that we moved into Mount Harold Terrace. In the meantime he grew weaker by the day. He continued to keep up his characteristically cheerful appearance. But the black marks under his eyes told a different story. He continued with his radio show and diocesan work as best he could. I was wishing that he was already in hospital seeking medical care.

On the Thursday before he went in he became particularly weak. His thyroid medication had been reduced and it was causing the weakness. I watched over him all that night, praying to God that he would be OK. He could hardly move his arms and legs and sat limply like a rag doll. The following morning I contacted his doctor and Michael was given medicine which improved his condition somewhat until it was time to go to the hospital. That day, before the doctor came, Michael sat at the table almost crouching over it, he was so weak. He had an A4 pad in front of him and began scribbling something down. He tore it out, coughing with the breath rasping in his throat, and handed it to me. I was too worried to bother reading any note and I stuffed it into my jeans. I didn't realise its significance for almost a year later.

The news of Michael's illness did not take long to spread through the right circles – even to Central America. On the morning of 28 August, the day before he went into hospital, the phone rang. I picked it up and said hello. 'How are you, Phyl?' came the unmistakably bubbly voice of Eamonn Casey. I recognised it the second he spoke. 'Hello, Eamonn, we haven't heard from you in a long time,' I said with a hint of sarcasm. 'Be God, now aren't you sharp,' he replied with a characteristic chuckle, surprised that I recognised his voice so quick. Michael was out and I told him to ring back that evening. When I told Michael he seemed surprised and stayed by the phone for the rest of the evening.

When Casey finally rang back, Michael took the call in the office. I was in the sitting-room, which is divided from the office by large partition doors. Suddenly I could hear Michael raise his voice almost to a scream. 'Why Eamonn, why, why, why didn't you tell me . . . Did you not trust me? Maybe I could have helped?' What I was hearing was breaking my heart. There was this explosion of emotions coming from Michael and he kept repeating the same question over and over again. He told Eamonn Casey how hurt and insulted he was when he hadn't called him during one of his secret trips into the country after the story broke. The conversation went on for about ten minutes and then there was silence from the room.

I got up and went into the office. Michael was sitting by the phone at his big mahogany desk. He was so upset and crying. I stood beside him and hugged him. All he could say was 'poor Eamonn, poor Eamonn'. There was no bitterness in Michael Cleary, he forgave everyone and had a big, generous heart. I don't know what Eamonn said to Michael except he said 'believe in God' to the dear friend he had let down. I was angry, damned angry, when I saw how upset Michael was. I wanted to say what was in my heart, that it had taken until Michael was seriously ill before he bothered picking up the phone, especially after everything that we had gone through. If there was one person in the world who would have known what the scandal had done to Michael it would have been Eamonn Casey. I have forgiven Eamonn for hurting the man I loved, Michael would have wanted me to. But I will never lose my sense of anger at him. Forgiveness has nothing to do with anger.

On the morning he went to the hospital, there was an air of apprehension in the house. We were all quiet and everyone was glum. Michael kept up the brave front and insisted that the three of us pose for photographs together. That was the one of Michael standing with his arms around us in the kitchen which appeared in the *Sunday World*. The only one attempting a smile was Michael. I was desperately fighting the tears which were welling up behind my eyes. I kept myself busy packing all his things and getting him ready. I didn't realise until some time later that Michael thought this was the last time he would ever be at home. Before he left he hugged Bonnie and the dogs.

Roisin, Ross and I took him to the hospital. It was a pleasant afternoon and the sun had broken through the clouds for the first time in a few days. It had been one of those typically damp Irish summers. When he was admitted we brought in his things and got him fixed up in his room. He joked and laughed with the nurses. But inside he was in despair. There were so many nurses around that I couldn't give him a hug and a kiss before leaving. I was so lonely and I could see it in his eyes. I couldn't say goodbye. As I was walking towards the car the tears began to flow. It was a painful parting I will never forget. I took his clothes home with me from the hospital. I put them under my pillow and slept with them there until he returned home.

He was kept in hospital until the Thursday of the following week. During those twelve days he was diagnosed as having cancer throughout his body. He began chemotherapy. Every day I went to see him. It was impossible to be with him by myself because of the sheer volume of visitors. His room was like Grand Central Station. In the end the nurses and doctors got concerned that Michael was having no time to rest. I would stand there with everyone else, the housekeeper coming to see how her employer was. No one would tell me what the doctor's prognosis was. I couldn't ask any questions because I wasn't a close relative. But every now and then our eyes would meet across the room, oblivious to the incessant chatter going on around us, and I could feel him saying: 'I love you.'

It was awful not being able to comfort him for fear that people would see us. I just wanted to hold him and say that everything was going to be all right and I couldn't. I had become accustomed to restraint in public through the past 26 years but this was torture. Standing at the edge of his bed surrounded by all those people was the loneliest place in the world. To make up for it he would call the house between five and ten times a day to talk to me and Ross. The first call would come between 7.30 and 9 a.m. and the last one anytime up to midnight. He was so lonesome in there. All he wanted to do was to be at home with us. Even though he was ill he never let down his guard on the phone. He would end the conversation by simply saying 'eight' – it was our secret code.

On the following Saturday morning, 4 September, I got up very early and went to the hospital before the inevitable influx of visitors. I got two buses to Mount Merrion and arrived just after 8.30 a.m. It was a warm morning and the sun was shining. As I walked up the drive to the hospital I spotted him sitting on a bench outside, in his dressing-gown, reading the newspaper.

As I walked towards him he looked up from it in my direction and then looked away. I got right up in front of him and stood there saying nothing. He continued to read the paper, totally unaware that I was there. My heart nearly stopped with fear.

'Don't you know me?' I asked nervously.

He got a jolt and looked up at me with a smile. 'Mother of God, what are you doing here this hour of the morning?'

'I wanted to come to see you when there was no other visitors . . . I just wanted a little while with you on my own,' I replied.

Then I told him that I didn't want him to lose his control over what was going on, not to give over his control to anyone else. In my heart I was scared all the time that, when he got out of hospital, someone else would take over looking after him and I would lose him. After all, I was only the housekeeper.

Our love was a forbidden secret and I did not have the rights of a partner or wife. I could not even enquire into what his real state of health was. In fact, at no stage during Michael's illness was I ever told his true state of health. Maybe it was for the better. In any event I was not a close relative. It was none of my business.

'I promise to keep my control and this is the nicest surprise I have had in a long time,' Michael said as he got up and folded the paper. Then he caught me gently by the arm and looked furtively over his shoulder.

'Have you got any fags with you . . . I'm gasping for a smoke, they don't like me smoking around here for some reason,' he grinned mischievously.

We went to his room and closed the door. We held each other tightly for a few precious minutes. He kissed me and sighed: 'Ah, it's so good to see you, Phyl. I wish I could just walk into the house and see Ross and the dogs and Bonnie.'

We sat on the bed and talked for about an hour. He was being very brave and optimistic. He said the doctor had told him that he wasn't riddled with cancer and he had a good chance of beating it this time, the same way he had before. I was elated by the news. As I went home, I was filled with hope and joy that everything was going to be all right. Later that day Ross, Roisin, Suzanne and I went back to see him. We brought him ice-cream and fruit which he had asked for. As usual the visitors were coming and going. That night around 10 p.m. he rang me again when he was at last free of visitors. 'It was really great to see you arrive this morning. Poets refer to it as the speir ban (meaning the vision),' he whispered down the line. I told him to get off the phone, that he needed rest because he still had a rough week ahead of him. 'OK,' he said, 'I will talk to you in the morning, 8!'

We spent the following Wednesday, 8 September, decorating the house with yellow ribbons for Michael's return the next afternoon. Ross, myself, Suzanne, Roisin and James put the ribbons everywhere, on the door handles, the stairs, his bed and even on his chair at the kitchen table. I had his room sparkling. I went with Denis Cleary, Michael's cousin, who owned the Dropping Well pub in Milltown, to bring him home. Michael and Denis were very close friends. When he came into the house he was groggy and weak but he got a great thrill to see the yellow ribbons. Before he left the hospital I was given a detailed chart of the medication Michael was to take at regular intervals through the day and night. I also kept a detailed record of everything he ate from then on.

On the first day I made a mistake and gave him two extra morphine tablets. When I discovered this I was frantic with worry that I had overdosed him. I rang the hospital almost in tears and the nurses told me that it would be all right and just to watch his breathing. The extra dosage made him more mellow. That evening members of his family came to visit, Mark Keohane, his nephew from Canada, Tom and Orla Cleary, Denis's children and Tom's fiancée. They stayed for an hour or so with Michael and left. Michael was very tired. I helped him upstairs to bed. When we were at the top of the first flight of stairs I said: 'My God, now I'm a nurse.' He looked into my eyes and replied: 'No, you are my everything.'

Shortly after he came home reporters got wind that he was ill and began calling the house. I told them that he was away and was fine. Michael continued doing his radio show and I said to him that he should be the one to break the news to his listeners and the bloody papers. One night during the show he revealed that the cancer had started again but, in typically robust style, said that he was going to beat it the same as he had before. After that we were inundated with calls from well-wishers. Michael was loved by a lot of people.

Four days after Michael came home Eamonn Casey again made contact. We got a call from one of Casey's sisters saying that he would be calling Michael from Central America early the following morning. I sat up with Michael on his bed as he waited for the call. I lay in his arms while he waited . . . and waited. At 4 a.m. Michael told me to go and get some sleep that he would wait on. I was so angry about that. Michael needed whatever rest he could get and here was Casey keeping him hanging on for a call all night. The following morning Michael said that he had to ring Eamonn instead because the call never came. He never told me what they talked about. It was the last time that they would ever speak to each other.

Gradually, Michael began to overcome the effects of the chemotherapy and started eating a little better every day. He went out visiting more often and to play cards with his friends. He was always in good spirits and didn't feel much pain. The toughest part was at night, sleeping with one eye open, listening to his coughing. But I never for one instant allowed myself to think that he wasn't going to beat it. But there were little signs which my optimism and hope blinded me to. The last time he got sick he went out and bought himself a new car. When I asked why he wasn't buying a new one this time he said: 'Sure there is nothing wrong with the one I have, it's only five years old and it will do me.' Before the illness he had planned to have teeth implants because his own teeth had fallen out. He was anxious to have it done. He used to laughingly say he needed an overhaul. Again he said that it could wait.

One thing Michael didn't want to delay was the renewal of the marriage vows we had exchanged all those years ago in the front room of his house in Marino. It was his suggestion. About a week after he came out of St Vincent's the three of us were sitting around the table in the kitchen. Michael casually suggested that we renew the vows in front of a small group of trusted people who knew our secret. Then we could go out for a meal, just the three of us, to celebrate. He asked Ross what he thought. Ross smiled and said: 'Ah, Father, that's soppy.' When a boy is 17, talk about marriage vows and the like are probably less than cool. I thought it was lovely, not only renewing vows but the way we were together. A loving family unit. I said to Michael that we could wait until he was better.

We began to go with the flow then because there wasn't much of a choice. I never stopped waiting and praying for the miracle to happen. He continued to go in and out of hospital for treatment and tests. We just waited, hoped and prayed. One of the most poignant moments was the day his hair started to fall out as a result of the chemotherapy, it was 20 September. He had been partially bald for years but the bit he had was wispy and he combed it across his head. Chunks and lumps of it started coming out on the comb. There was a deep sadness. A sadness that you would rather endure yourself than watch someone you deeply loved going through. I was helpless. It was like reality suddenly kicking down the door. His beard disappeared and within a short time he was left with a few strands. A lot of people didn't know him to see. Michael was very depressed when he saw it falling out. I tried to boost his morale.

'Look at Jean Luc Picard, the character on *Star Trek*, he has no hair and yet is one of the sexiest men in the world. So is Sean Connery. It doesn't matter if you have no hair,' I told him. To me Michael's changed appearance meant nothing. When you are in love with someone the way I was, you are not looking for beauty, you are looking at the person you love. The part you fall in love with is the part that no one can see.

Most years Michael travelled with a group of people to Lourdes, in France. He really loved it there and had booked the trip before he became ill. Now he had a greater reason than ever to make the pilgrimage that he cherished so much. Michael wanted me to go with him. He said that I would love it. In hindsight, I think Michael deep down inside felt that this would be our last trip together. I agreed to go. He went to see his doctors and they gave him the all clear to travel. There were some people on the trip I couldn't get on with and Michael knew this. Even though he was sick, he made sure that the people concerned went on a different flight and stayed in a different hotel to avoid friction. Peg O'Connell also came on the trip and we shared a room together. Both Michael and I were filled with optimism getting on that flight. I still clung to the belief that the dream I had was a warning and that he would recover.

The trip was from 2 October to 7 October. The flight was to go at 7 p.m. in the evening but was delayed for four hours. Michael was very tired and it was arranged for him and a few of us to go to the executive suite where we watched television until the plane was ready. It was around 4 a.m. when we finally booked into our hotel, the Alba in Lourdes. Peg and I shared a room next to Michael's. The next day we went to Mass in this little convent called St Clare's. It was pouring with rain and Michael went back up to bed for a nap. Everyone in the hotel knew him and loved him and made sure he wanted for nothing. Then the rest of the group went on a tour of the places St Bernadette – the girl to whom the Blessed Virgin had appeared – had lived. She is my heroine. Bernadette was persecuted because she told the truth to all those who disbelieved her.

Michael was right, it is one of the most beautiful places on God's earth, although you have to close your eyes to the commercial side of it. It fills the soul full of joy and happiness. Michael was in great form. At night when our group came back to the hotel from the grotto he stayed up playing cards and singing songs. On the second day the sun came out and it was really uplifting. I felt so happy there, especially seeing Michael enjoy himself so much. Lourdes is such a wonderfully holy place. Most of the time we were near each other but I kept a respectable distance because I didn't want to draw attention to us. He spent much of the time in the company of an old golfing partner of his, Harry Cullen.

Every now and then across a crowded room or on a tour Michael would give me a wink. We made love twice during the trip, on the third and last nights. Before he went to bed he would say 'pop in to see me before you go to sleep' making sure he did so well out of earshot. He wanted his arms around me and I wanted mine around him. When we were in bed he held me tighter than he ever did, even though he was so fragile. When we made love it was intense. Like it was the last time. When he fell asleep I would go back to my own room. Those nights remain dear to my heart. Everyone really enjoyed the trip and we all, including Michael, planned to make the trip again in 1994. Michael wanted Ross to come the next time. He said it would be our first holiday together as a family. He was also really looking forward to 1994. He had pencilled in the dates of the Irish World Cup matches and intended travelling to the US with Ross for at least one of the games.

One night after we came back from Lourdes I was in the room with Michael, talking. He told me that he wanted to make some financial arrangements for Ross and me in the event that he didn't make it. I was distraught and refused to talk about it. I cried and he cradled me in his arms. I couldn't talk about Michael's death in any way. I was living in hope that everything would turn out all right. Around the same time Fr. Brian Darcy called at the house to see Michael. We were sitting in the kitchen talking about everything and anything when Michael told Brian: 'You know, Brian, that you are residual executor of the will.' Then Michael looked at me and said: 'That is the way that it has to be done.' When Michael died we never saw Brian Darcy again.

Kathleen, Michael's sister, was home on holiday from Canada and Michael planned to have a luncheon for his immediate family and some friends. Michael really wanted everything to go smoothly. He asked a relation to prepare the food and said that he would tell his sisters that it was me. He was very anxious that I looked good in their eyes. The luncheon was held in the house on Friday, 22 October. There were about 20 people in the house and everything went fine. Afterwards Michael celebrated Mass. The following evening I went to a cabaret show in Clontarf Castle with Patricia and Kathleen. It was a relatively enjoyable evening but I felt that there was some tension in the air. Then on Sunday something happened which again threw Michael and myself into crisis.

A member of the family found out that Roisin had called the Archbishop's house a second time, a few weeks earlier, to repeat the allegation about Ross. This time she identified herself. She knew what everyone else did except Ross and me, that Michael was dying. She wanted something done to ensure Ross and I were all right after his death. I knew nothing about the second trip and when I heard about it I was very upset. There was a big row and Michael went to a family meeting which had been arranged to discuss the claims. I was so worried when Michael told me where he was going. While he was away at the meeting I cried a lot.

When he arrived home much later, he was downhearted. He said that he had discussed the claims with his family but he wouldn't go into any great detail about what transpired. I didn't want to hear anymore anyway. I wanted him to be okay and beat this thing which was eating him up inside. 'When you are well and finished your chemo treatments we can deal with this . . . it's not important at the moment,' I told him. Whatever happened at that meeting upset Michael. I could see him brooding about it from time to time after that.

As Christmas approached Michael continued his chemotherapy and seemed to be holding his own. He insisted that the house be redecorated. I argued that he should leave it until his treatment was over early in the new year. I was afraid that the disruption and the paint fumes would make him sick. But he was having none of it. We planned for Christmas. My niece and nephew, Emma Lee and Mark, were going to come over from London for the holidays. Michael loved them. He loved having children around the house. He was like a big, generous uncle to the lot of them. On Christmas Day we were going to Patricia's for dinner, just like we did every year.

On the Tuesday of Christmas week, 21 December, Denis Cleary died suddenly. The news of his death shocked and deeply saddened Michael. He loved the man. The weather was bitterly cold, something which greatly concerned me because with the chemotherapy, Michael's immunity system had broken down and he was at risk of catching pneumonia. On Christmas Eve Michael performed the sad task of officiating at Denis's funeral. He was feeling poorly and couldn't seem to get warm. After the Mass I went home to my niece and nephew. Later, I discovered that after the burial Michael drove into town and bought me my Christmas present, a video recorder. It would be the last gift he ever got me.

When he arrived home he was cold and weary. I could see the sadness in his eyes. I had his electric duvet on full and he went to bed for a while. When he got up he was visibly unwell. He would only eat tea and toast and that worried me. I sat beside him at the table and told him that he was in no fit state to go to the radio. He looked into my eyes: 'I know I'm not able, I will get Larry Hogan to fill in for me.' It was unusual to hear Michael agree that he wasn't able to go to the radio although I was glad that he was staying in out of the cold. He took a few more phone calls and had a few callers. At 10 p.m. he went to bed after having a bowl of soup. I gave him his prescribed sleeping pill and checked on him every few minutes after that.

After midnight I heard him stirring in his room next door and jumped out of bed. He had to go to the bathroom a lot and I was nervous that he might fall down the stairs. When I heard him going back to bed I decided to sit up. I took a patchwork quilt from my bed and sat outside his room. Every time he stirred to go to the bathroom I would switch off my light so that he didn't know I was keeping an eye on him. He settled down around 5.30 a.m. and seemed to sleep.

I came downstairs, made some tea and watched the Christmas morning news on Sky. It was full of good news and seasonal cheer, though I couldn't feel it. At 7.30 a.m. Michael arrived down. 'I'd rather be down here in your company than up there on my own,' he said as he lay on the couch in the kitchen. He looked absolutely worn out and I put a few pillows under his head and a duvet over him. It wasn't long before he had to go to the toilet again. I called his GP and asked him to come down because I was concerned about Michael. When he came back down from the bathroom he coughed and I could see that his tongue was quite coated. I got a toothbrush and a bowl and tried to clean it. He suddenly vomited what looked like bile. Alarm bells went off in my head and I immediately called his oncologist and told him Michael needed to be in hospital.

He rang back and said a room was ready on the first floor in St Vincent's. I called Orla Cleary, Denis's daughter, and she came round to drive us to the hospital. Then I rang Michael's GP and cancelled my earlier call. I threw on a track suit and sneakers. I didn't wash my face and forgot to put on my socks. Michael was so weak he could hardly talk. I got a bag ready for him and put some heavy clothes on him. It took us a matter of minutes to get to the hospital, the streets were completely deserted. It was a dark, damp morning. As we sped past the houses with their twinkling Christmas lights I envied all those people who were going to have a happy, peaceful day. For a moment my mind wandered back to all the lovely Christmases we had together.

When we got Michael settled into his bed in St Vincent's I felt good that he was in professional hands. The nurses took blood and did other tests to find out what had caused the vomiting. He was very lethargic and was in and out to the commode every half hour or so. Outside the room window a carpet of magpies fluttered around the lawn and I thought to myself: 'There's too many of them for one for sorrow, two for joy. It must mean something good.' I craved for signs to give me hope. I stayed with him all that day. I talked to Ross on the phone several times. He was very worried about his father and I reassured him that everything was going to be fine. Michael's sister Patricia came in with two cousins and stayed for a while. Another one of Michael's cousins brought me in some dinner in the late afternoon.

The nurses and doctors were very tolerant all day until about a dozen visitors came in and then they asked the lot of us to leave. Before I left, Michael asked me to bring Ross in to see him. I went home to our son and my niece and nephew, exhausted and worried. I began praying like I'd never prayed before. I would have given anything to hear the words 'Its only a temporary setback'. The kids were confused at all the commotion. Ross was worrying about his father but I convinced him that everything was OK and he could go to see him the next day.

On St Stephen's Day I brought Ross in with me to see Michael. He was delighted to see his son. In the 24 hours that had passed he had gone downhill rapidly. He was so weak. Michael and Ross spent a while alone together talking. All along Ross had been like me, clinging to hope that Michael would pull through, refusing to believe that anything would happen to him. When he left I was on my own with Michael. The cancer was destroying him in front of my very eyes. It was as if he was failing by the minute. At that moment I wished that it was me instead of him. Ross needed a father now more than a mother. God couldn't take this wonderful man away from us. He had no right.

I sat down on the edge of the bed. Michael was lying on his right side. Tears were streaming down his cheeks. 'Thank you so much for bringing Ross in to see me,' he whispered. He threw his left arm around me and kissed me on the lips. It was a cold kiss, his whole body was cold. His body was dying but his spirit, his love, was very much alive.

'You'll never know how much I love you,' he said. 'Oh, I do my love, I do,' I whispered back. Even at this, the lowest stage in our lives together, here on a hospital bed with the life draining from Michael's body, we were still being cautious in case anyone walked in and saw us. I shouldn't have cared less who saw us.

'You didn't get your Christmas present. Take the keys of the car out of the locker and tell Ross to get it out of the boot.' The instruction knocked me for six. He was thinking of my present when all he should have been thinking of was his health.

'It doesn't matter now. It can wait until you come home and then you can give it to me yourself.' I rubbed his brow. But he insisted and I took the keys. I left shortly after that and went home with Ross. That was the last time I ever kissed Michael Cleary.

The next day, Monday 27 December, I visited Michael in the hospital twice. He was deteriorating very rapidly. I wanted to spend as much time as possible by his side. When I got home Patricia rang me and said that the family had agreed that no one would go in to see him for the next while. He was to be given space so that he could recover. I wholeheartedly agreed. I would do anything to speed up his recovery as I desperately clung to hope. She said that a 'nurse delegate' had been appointed to ring every morning to give us an update on how he was.

Over the next day I couldn't relax or sleep. I paced the floor watching the phone. I rang the nurses every few hours to see how he was. Then, on Wednesday evening, Michael rang me. I was so surprised but delighted to hear his voice. He was groggy but sounded lonesome, like he had been abandoned. I was almost fighting with him for making the call. 'You are supposed to be resting up and getting well.' When I put the phone down I cried and cried. Then I said to myself 'to hell with this I am going to see him no matter what anyone says'.

I got on the phone to his doctor, John Crown. I said I wanted him to put it down on Michael's chart that I was allowed to visit and not to be stopped. I said I didn't want arguments with staff or anyone else but I was going to see Michael no matter what. He agreed and said that as far as he was concerned Michael wasn't terminal. I was relieved and slept a little that night.

When I got up the next morning, Thursday 30 December, the light on the answering machine was flashing. When I switched it on I could hear Michael's voice mumbling something and the voice of a nurse saying, 'Father, what are you doing with the phone, give it to me. You need to rest now.'

I felt I had to get to the hospital straightaway but, for some reason, waited for the nurse delegate to call. She called at 9.45 a.m. She said that she did not like the look of Michael and that she had been on to his sisters to inform them that we were all to go to the hospital. Michael was fading fast. He was slipping away from me and I could do nothing. I wasn't able to cry I was so numb.

I had to wait for a member of the family to pick me up. It seemed like an eternity before they arrived. When I got to the hospital, the rest of Michael's family were there. Michael was starting to die. Death had begun its merciless process of taking my love away. His eyes were bulging and his stomach bloated. He was lucid for only short periods. I begged God not to take him. I was standing by his bed when he woke up out of his semi-conscious state. He said: 'I thought I saw Muriel and Patricia here, where are they?' he asked. I said: 'We are all here together, we are just waiting for you to get well again.' He looked up at me, his eyes half closing and whispered: 'You know something? You're great . . . I love you.' Then he went to sleep again.

As the day wore on he was becoming more and more distressed. Ross arrived for a while. He was confused and distressed. I know he wanted to be at his father's side. After a while he asked me if I minded if he went home and I said no. He said: 'I'll just go to see the nurse and tell her if Father wakes up to tell him we all love him and can't wait for him to get better.' As he walked out of the waiting room one of Michael's relations said she preferred if he didn't go in. Ross just looked at me. That expression of sadness and hurt on his face is one I will never forget. The poor child was lost.

When we came home Ross and I sat hugging each other. I cried for my son. None of this was fair on him. He never asked to be born into such a bizarre world. After Ross went to bed I stayed up. I called the hospital through the night but there had been no change. About 5.15 a.m. I rang again to be told that he was agitated but resting. I lay down on my bed in a state of despair. How could he rest if he was agitated? I cried as memories of our life together flooded through my mind like a fast flowing river. I tried to connect with him and closed my eyes. I fell into some kind of drowsy state. I thought: 'Michael, you have suffered dreadfully, don't keep holding on if you want to go home. Give in and go to God. Ross and I will be OK. Just don't go on suffering on our account.'

The phone interrupted my thoughts. It was a nurse. She said that there was someone on the way to pick me up. Michael was critical. I got up and dressed faster than lightning. I woke Ross up. He must have slept in his clothes because he was at the door in seconds, waiting for Darriel, Michael's niece, to arrive. The child was in a state of panic. He was losing the most important person in the world, his father. The man he adored. It was 6 a.m. as we drove through the deserted, darkened streets. My thoughts and my eyes were focused on getting to Michael. I was shaking. 'Oh, please don't leave. God, please don't take him away,' I prayed.

As we got to the elevator Patricia met us. She put her arm around me and said the words which shattered my world forever. 'He's gone.' I think I screamed something like 'Oh no, please no.' I wanted to go to him and drag him back into life. Ross collapsed onto his knees. He was pale. Tears began trickling down his face. I cried for Michael's soul as it made its way to a happier place. A place where he would find peace. A place where he wouldn't have to live the lie anymore, where there were no prying eyes. Then I thought about the fear he had lived with since May 1992 that we would be exposed by the media. 'At least no one can hurt him anymore.'

CHAPTER 11

Journey Through Hell

FROM THE MOMENT Michael breathed his last, Ross and I began a long, lonely journey through hell which would seem to last forever. When we had composed ourselves and dried our tears that morning in the hospital we were brought to Michael's room with the rest of the family. He looked peaceful lying there in pyjamas. I couldn't believe that he was dead and expected him to wake up any minute and crack a joke. My stomach was in a knot. The pyjamas, light purple and white, were used by all of us when he was alive and we were a family. I often wore the top as a nightdress and other times Ross wore it as a shirt. Poor Michael would often be left with just the bottoms. There were many humorous tiffs over who was wearing Michael's pyjamas.

The hardest thing was adjusting to using the past tense when I talked about him. During those first days when I changed 'is' to 'was' a lump formed in my throat as if to stop me using the word. It was all so final. I began to feel so alone and scared. Shortly after the prayers were over Patricia informed me that Michael was to be laid out in his vestments and to ensure that I had them cleaned. I rushed home and got everything ready. I didn't have time to think. I was working on automatic. I could have been getting one of his suits ready for another function or retreat. I went back to the hospital with Suzanne and left the vestments with a nurse. Ross stayed at home, alone with his thoughts. Peg O'Connell was at the hospital and she came back with us.

It was around 11 a.m. when I got back to the house and I was surprised to find Patricia with her daughter Michelle and Tom Cleary in Michael's office clearing out his desk. They were filling large industrial sacks full of documents and files. Then a workman was brought in and helped remove the filing cabinet. It was taken away in a van and they left. For the rest of the day the house was full. Friends and members of the clergy came and went. Everyone was so upset.

Later that day as I was saying goodbye to one group of people another friend of Michael's, a former parishioner, was coming in. Just as she was coming through the door I saw Tom Cleary arrive back at the house. I thought he was coming in. Instead, he talked to someone briefly at the gate, turned and opened Michael's car and drove it away. I never saw it again. Amid the pain and anguish, I couldn't figure out what was going on. It gave me a bad feeling.

The removal and funeral was the worst part. Saying goodbye to the man I had shared all my adult life with was heartbreaking. He was my husband, my lover, the father of my children, my friend and mentor. We had been through so much together. We had a lot of happy times and plenty of bad times. I still can't help believing that in the end it was the fear of being exposed which caused his cancer to recur. I was a widow, but because of a callous Church with its archaic, superficial morality, I couldn't be his widow. In a more enlightened world Michael would have been an inspiration to the Catholic Church. He was probably one of the few men in the world who honoured his obligations to both sides of his life.

On Tuesday 4 January we buried Michael alongside his parents in Mulhuddart cemetery following noon Mass in St Brigid's Church in Blanchardstown. I personally felt that he would have preferred a simple funeral in a large church to accommodate the huge crowds who came to pay their last respects to the man they loved and admired. The church was too small and a large crowd had to stand outside in the cold. There were newspaper photographers and a TV crew there. Even at his funeral I had to act like some kind of criminal, keeping my head down in case I drew attention. I felt a little awkward when people came up and sympathised with me, some of them either knew our secret or had certainly suspected for many years.

As they lowered his coffin into the ground I could feel my soul going down there with him. My whole body literally ached with the pain of losing him. A part of me was dying too. I wanted to be with him but I needed to be with my son, our son, the product of our love for each other. We lived our lives in secret, now we would have to grieve in secret. As they tossed the frozen earth down into that hole in the ground I wanted to cry out but I couldn't. Even at the lowest, most heartbreaking moment in my miserable life, I had to be careful. How angry that makes me feel today. But I felt a little comfort from those close friends of Michael's, the people who knew our secret, who I felt would support Ross and me. At the graveside their handshakes were strong, their hugs reassuring. They would help me get through this terrible time.

After the funeral friends drove Ross and me home. I wanted to be at home to comfort our son and I declined an invitation from the family to join them for a meal. We have never been to the grave since. It would be just too much to bear. There were quite a few visitors all afternoon. When they had gone my sister told me that my friends wanted to take me out for a drink. At first I didn't want to but eventually gave in. As I was waiting for them I phoned a member of Michael's family and left a message that I was going out. We were just about to go out through the door when the phone rang. It was a member of the family. She was frantic. 'Thank God you are still there, Michael's sisters are coming to see you now.' I told my friends and sister to go ahead without me. I hadn't an idea

175

what was going on. Then the doorbell rang. I opened it, surprised to see Tom Cleary standing there followed by Muriel, Kathleen, Patricia and Marita. They appeared cool and distant. I made tea for them and then it was down to business.

Tom Cleary took out a white envelope from his inside pocket. It had already been opened. It was Michael's will. This totally threw me. I could not believe they could be doing this when he was hardly cold in his grave. It was the last thing I was thinking about. I felt alone and helpless amid people who, in the past few days, had grown distant towards me. Tom read it out in a cold, dispassionate voice. It read:

I, Father Michael Cleary, make this my final and absolute will for the disposal of my worldly goods and possessions. I declare on this the 25th day of September, 1992, that I am of sound mind and acting without any pressure from anyone.

I leave £100 each to all my nieces and nephews trusting that they will realise that I gave them all I could while alive.

I have a house in Finglas at present occupied rent-free by the Brigidine Nuns. I leave this house to the Archdiocese of Dublin. The deeds are in the possession of Irish Nationwide Building Society and there is a mortgage on the house, but a profit should accrue to the Archdiocese.

I have a house in Bayview Avenue, North Strand. This is fully owned by me and has been let out rent-free to various occupants since I purchased it. I leave this house to my housekeeper, Phyllis Hamilton, and her son Ross Hamilton. I also leave all my household goods and furniture to Phyllis Hamilton, trusting that she will give my sisters some pieces and objects that might be of sentimental value to them.

I leave £500 to the Passionists Fathers in Mount Argus to offer 100 Masses for my intentions.

The residue, if any, of my property, moneys, shares, goods, I leave to Fr. Brian Darcy of the *Sunday World* to disperse at his own discretion to charity.

The deeds of the house in Bayview Avenue are in the offices of Cathal Young Solicitors, 1 Lr. Leeson Street. I appoint as my executors Thomas Cleary, Dropping Well, Milltown. Fr. James Tormey, CC, Narraghmore, Co. Kildare.

Signed Michael Cleary PP.

As soon as the reading was over Michael's sisters went around the house taking mementos of their brother, in accordance with the will. They took the Waterford crystal which adorned the shelves in the sitting-room. They hardly spoke to me. The atmosphere was very tense. I sat on the side of a chair in the kitchen, crying as they went about their business. I asked James, our loyal friend, to go up to the sitting-room and try to put some order back into it. But that was all he could do. From that moment on the spirit and the warmth of that once special room was gone. The Christmas tree, its lights switched off, was a sorry, lonely sight in the corner. Our once happy home had become a cold, lonely house.

A few days later Tom Cleary arrived back with Patricia and Marita. They had a cup of tea, and again the atmosphere was tense and then Tom asked me if it was all right if he took some of Michael's suits. I took him upstairs and the others followed. They took away the clerical gear hanging in Michael's wardrobe. I felt they had taken enough of him.

The following Friday a *News of the World* reporter knocked on the door. Luckily I did not answer it and he was told I wasn't at home. He came back in the evening and was told the same. He muttered something about Fr. Pat Buckley and Michael. At the time Buckley was suing 98 FM over comments Michael made about him on his radio show. Memories of 1992 began flooding back into my tormented mind. I could only sit and wait to see the paper to find out what exactly they were up to. A few days later Patricia came to visit. She was in a belligerent mood. I was alone with her in the kitchen when she came in. Sue and Ross listened from Michael's office. She said she did not accept that Michael was Ross's father and therefore I should agree to swearing an affidavit that someone else was Ross's father. I couldn't believe what she was saying to me. I replied: 'Do you know exactly what an affidavit is?' The conversation didn't last very long and she left without another word.

I felt I needed help. Before Michael died he left the name of the Archbishop's staff, Monsignor Gerry Sheehy. He said I should contact the monsignor if the need arose. I also reckoned that they would be able to help because they had been informed of the situation on several occasions by Roisin O'Shea. Monsignor Sheehy visited the house and listened to my story. He was friendly and reassuring. I told him that I needed to move out of Mount Harold Terrace. I also wanted advice on what to do about the media. He left me his phone number and the name of a solicitor I was to contact. A short time after he left, Monsignor Sheehy rang back to give me the name of another lawyer. 'The first guy must have known what he was getting himself into,' he told me. The second solicitor was quite happy to look after our interests.

Then the storm came and the nightmare we had always feared, began. It was Wednesday night, 12 January 1994. I got a call from Orla Cleary, Tom's sister, telling me that she had heard there was going to be something in the *Phoenix* magazine the following morning. I was shaking with apprehension of what was to come. The next morning we sent James out to the shop to buy a copy as soon as it arrived. It carried the story that Michael had been a father. It referred in accurate detail, to myself and Ross and aspects of our life with him. When I saw it I was physically sick. I was consumed with anger and sheer hate for whoever it was who had sunk so low to divulge this information. I could have committed murder.

From that moment on, while things were bleak and lonely, our lives were turned into hell. It was what we, all three of us, had prepared for in 1992. But now Michael was not there to stand with us. Our well-laid plans were useless without him. We packed most of our belongings in case we had to get out fast. If I had the money I would have used the passports Michael hastily arranged to take my son away from all of this. Instead, we locked ourselves away behind drawn curtains, like fugitives. When Ross got up and read the magazine he went pale. The poor child was in a state of utter shock and despair. As he walked into the front sitting-room he spotted a photographer across the road aiming a long-range lens at him. He dived to the floor like he was being shot at. The siege had begun.

The media were relentless. Like an army on the offensive they came in their droves. Banging on the door, ringing the phone. The questions were aggressive. They demanded answers. As I crouched in a room inside behind a locked door, I was pulverised with fear. Sue and James had always been there for us. They were like part of our family and they loved Michael like they were his children. When Michael was dying James offered to have one of his lungs transplanted just so as the man he loved and admired could live. Although nervous and deeply upset, they faced the hungry newspaper people. That was when we decided to refer all queries about the affair to Michael's sisters. Michael's large number of celebrity friends were being interviewed in every newspaper in the country condemning the *Phoenix* and denying that Michael had fathered a child. At the time I agreed with them.

Our solicitor came to meet with Ross and me on Friday. He was very nice and understanding towards us. Before he came I rang Monsignor Sheehy and asked if I should deny everything. He told me to 'tell the truth' and not deny anything. I felt like a five-year-old child scared of the busy traffic, with no one to take me across the road. I was prepared to make a statement to the newspapers denying the story in the *Phoenix*, but we were advised against that. Later that evening the solicitor rang back to tell me that the Archbishop's house had heard a member of my family had sold my story to the *Sunday World*. I was in shock and disbelief that a member of my own family would do such a thing. I rang each one and had to ask the very ugly question. Of course none of them had talked to anybody. They were hurt that I had seemed to doubt them.

I arranged to meet my solicitor the next morning to see what we could do about the paper. Sue drove me into town. We went to the church on Clarendon Street. I prayed to Michael to give me strength to get through this nightmare. Then, in a café, I had a glass of milk and several more cigarettes before going to the solicitor's offices. We waited for a while for a senior counsel to arrive. We went through everything and he asked if I wanted to seek an injunction against the *Sunday World*. I didn't really know what an injunction entailed and I didn't know what was supposed to be in the paper in the first place. Both the counsel and my solicitor agreed that I would only be throwing myself head first into the media's hands. We decided to wait and see what was going to appear.

It was a long day's wait until the Sunday papers hit the street that night. When the *Sunday World* came in it had a short piece about me allegedly trying to commit suicide. I was angry about it, but it wasn't the story I had feared. But then it became obvious that somehow we had been sent on a wild goose chase. The *Sunday Tribune* carried an astonishing front page story which deeply distressed both Ross and me. Under the headline, 'Fr. Cleary's family "to prove" innocence', Tom Cleary made claims which completely shattered me.

He claimed that the family had evidence which would completely disprove allegations that he had fathered a child. Tom claimed that they had affidavits from two men stating that they were the fathers of my two sons. He also claimed that Michael had taken a DNA test in London as part of his proof that the allegations were untrue. He went on to claim that Michael had undergone the tests in 1992 following claims that he had fathered a child. To my utter disbelief Tom went on to state that these documents were being examined by the family's solicitor and were actually going to be released to the media 'soon'.

He directly referred to Ross by claiming that the DNA test would prove Michael was not his father. He said that Michael had gone to these two unidentified men and obtained statements from them saying they were the fathers of the two boys. He claimed that Michael had merely counselled me in the past. I was speechless. I cried and cried for days. Ross was devastated. I could see the anger and confusion in his young face. He didn't say much. At first he felt betrayed that his father could do such a thing. But neither of us accepted that Michael would do such a thing. He was very confused and upset but I thanked God for the scientist who discovered DNA testing. My lawyers have since requested these alleged DNA tests and both Ross and I have made it quite clear through our legal representatives that we are prepared to undergo DNA tests ourselves in a bid to clarify the issue.

The next time I spoke to Tom Cleary was when he came by with his mother on their way to Michael's month's mind Mass. He stayed for only a few minutes. I said I wouldn't be going. Then I looked Tom in the eye and told him the damage the article had done to us. 'You have hurt me but you have hurt Ross even more. I can't believe what was said about us.' He didn't reply and left without another word. We never met him again.

In the following days there were more denials from prominent people in the media. Everyone was shooting off at the mouth about us. But none of them stopped for a second to think that there was a deeply troubled young man out there who had been crushed by all this. And amid all the furore we noticed how so many people began to put a safe distance between them and us. People who knew our secret suddenly developed amnesia. Some people we considered our friends did not want to have anything to do with us. Others came to see us just to find out if there was a risk that we were going to talk to the newspapers.

Archbishop Desmond Connell sent a letter to the priests of the Diocese a few days after the story in the *Tribune*. It read:

> Recent reports concerning the late Father Michael Cleary will have caused pain, anger and embarrassment to priests and people in the diocese and throughout Ireland.
>
> My policy in responding to these reports has been guided by my concern both for the good name of Father Cleary and for those closely affected by the reports.
>
> I want you and your parishioners to know of my concern for you at this time.
>
> I am confident that with God's help this ordeal can renew and deepen our sense of solidarity and of what it means in today's world to be together, the disciples of Christ.

Then in March, I started getting very upsetting filthy phone calls from someone I didn't know. A man's voice called me a slut and a whore and many other dreadful things. One night the voice screamed down the line at me: 'You bitch, you bitch, I hope you are lonely, you slut you deserve to die.' Ross even suffered the wrath of the evil caller and it really upset him. I was horrified. Then I was threatened that if I didn't stay silent we could be 'got at' by former prisoners in Mountjoy who had been fond of Michael. This terrified me. Every time Ross went out I was scared that something might happen to him.

The story about us just won't seem to go away. On 27 April at a function in the National Concert Hall the MIR award from the Families in Need group was given in recognition of Michael's work on behalf of his parishioners. Muriel and Patricia accepted the award for Michael. The next morning's papers carried quotes from a priest at the ceremony. He told the assembled audience: 'An awful lot of people were upset by the rumours which sprang up after his death. We believe that a terrible wrong was done to him and we would like to honour him.'

In the meantime there were other urgent problems, this time over money, or the lack of it. When Michael died I was left with virtually nothing except my unmarried mother's allowance which Michael had insisted that I continue to collect. The will had not yet been admitted to probate and I was left virtually penniless. When the gas, electricity and phone bills began falling on the mat I was panic-stricken. Michael was always extravagant when it came to utilities. He loved lots of light and heat and he never got off the phone. He would say: 'Don't worry about the bills . . . if money was our only worry we would have no worries at all.' The ESB bill was almost £200, the phone close to £500 and the gas over £300.

When the final notices started coming I found myself not knowing which way to turn. Eventually Monsignor Sheehy made arrangements whereby the diocese would make the payments. In one telephone conversation with the monsignor I discussed my sheer frustration at the situation I found myself in. The call was inadvertently taped on the answering machine. He was anxious to know if I had been approached by the media about the story and I said I had but I hadn't entertained them. Then I said maybe I had done the wrong thing. 'Not at all, not at all. All these people [the media] are looking for is to make money themselves . . . that is all there is to it, they are not in the slightest bit interested in you,' he told me. I said that I was prepared to take my secret to the grave. 'Oh, and that would be the place for it, Phyl,' he replied.

I had to begin economising and cutting back. It was a particularly tough time on Ross because his father gave him as much money as he wanted. He had never taught his son to save, with the result that Ross had no conception about how to handle money. He had never seen a time when there was a scarcity of pocket money. I got the gas fireplace taken out of the sitting-room and bought bits and pieces of fuel so that we could at least have a fire in the evenings. A neighbour chopped down a tree and gave it to us. We only used electricity when it was absolutely necessary and the phone was kept for urgent calls only. We used the gas twice daily to heat the water and I began to use a hot-water bottle. I had some savings which kept food on the table.

Our lives changed drastically. I got up every morning without much heat and did my chores. Ross finally gave up school. He could not concentrate and felt that he had become an object of intense curiosity and taunts. Then there was the confusion and anxiety of what our futures held. We were in a state of limbo. We had no money and the situation wasn't changing. Then there was the constant fear of the media and those anonymous threats. I had also asked the Archbishop's house to give us some place of equal value to the house left to us in Michael's will so that we could begin living somewhere else and blend into the background. We locked ourselves away from the outside world. Our once happy home had become our prison.

There was correspondence between my solicitor and Tom Cleary's solicitor to get a copy of the will. His instructions to his legal representatives was that he was fearful that the will 'would be leaked to the newspapers'. One day when I was looking through some old papers I found a letter Michael had addressed to me. It was typed with the date 16 October, 1993. Apparently he wrote it after trying to tell me that he was not hopeful of beating the cancer. In those months I clung so desperately to hope that I was deaf to such words. But he knew at that stage he was dying and he wanted to ensure we were looked after when he was gone. In it Michael left details of how we could gain access to an off-shore bank account in the Isle of Man.

In the letter he said: 'I realise now that it is difficult for you to think about my death. However, it is something we all have to face and I am being realistic enough to face the reality of the odds against me beating this illness the second time around, that is why I brought up the subject, it was not to cause you upset of any kind.

'I could go at any given time, even in a crash or from a heart attack, anything or anyone of a dozen reasons and I just want you to be prepared. You will have to know what to do for yourself and Ross in that eventuality.' The letter said he had left a letter with detailed instructions in the filing cabinet which, he said, I was to bring to an accountant friend of his. 'He is there to advise you . . . I know he will look after you both,' he wrote. There were also details of racehorses and a reference to share certificates. I haven't been able to find that letter.

The letter ended: 'I wish I could have discussed this with you today, in a calm manner, but I could see that your optimism was more important than a discussion filled with doom and gloom. Make sure that Ross knows I love him and take good care of each other. The last couple of years have been hard on all of us, I do not think I will make it. As I said in the beginning I must consider the odds. Make a life for yourselves when I am no longer here and I hope and pray you will be happy.'

I stared at the letter for hours. I cried as I thought of the pain it must have caused Michael to write those sad words of farewell. He was right, I couldn't have discussed death with him, I couldn't let my hope fade. But I was also confused and angry. Where was this money, if it existed as Michael's letter suggested it did, all this time we had been living like veritable paupers. We were at the mercy of the Church which could stop paying the bills at any time, which they did in June of 1995.

* * *

The days dragged into weeks, and then months, without anything happening. Not knowing what our futures held was devastating. We were between hell and limbo. Ross was my main concern. This was destroying him. He was the innocent one. And now he was being punished for the actions of his father. No matter how much I tried to comfort him, Ross felt like some kind of freak of nature who was universally denied. He loved his father the same as any other son does. He was proud of him. But he wasn't allowed to express that pride or to be acknowledged. He couldn't settle at anything because he was so ill-at-ease. He got a few part-time jobs.

On a number of occasions, in a fit of desperation, he threatened to get on his bike and cycle out to RTE to tell the world who he was, but I managed to stop him. Every day he would ask me what I was going to do. It was like he was pleading with me to take action, to end this journey through hell. I would beg him to be patient. That I would do something when the time was right. I could see the emotions building up inside him, ready to erupt at any moment. I was scared for him and lived in dread that he might do something drastic, like take his own life. Then, during a conversation, Ross told me that he had felt like committing suicide and leaving letters for the newspapers. I called Ivor Browne on a few occasions and he came to see us. He, too, was most concerned. Ivor also visited the diocese to discuss his concerns about the situation. I knew that time was running out for us. I would have to do something soon.

That was when I began considering going public with our story. It was something in my wildest dreams, I once would not have considered. But in my worst dreams I could not have envisaged the hell my son and I were about to go through. In November 1994 I felt that my solicitor had done everything he could for us and we parted on good terms. Some time later, a friend suggested I go to a relation of his, Peter Lennon, of Lennon Heather and Company on Mespil Road. Ross and I went to see him shortly after that. He immediately agreed to take on what was a particularly difficult and rather bizarre case. Over the next few months Peter was to become a dear friend to both of us. He is a man with a deep-rooted sense of justice. As a lawyer he is a formidable ally.

Peter agreed that I should go public and undertook to make enquiries as to what journalist or newspaper I should talk to. He was anxious that our story would be treated fairly and responsibly. Money was not a consideration. Going public was the only option left open to me. In January while I was sorting through old papers I found a letter which *Sunday World* journalist Paul Williams put through my door after the appearance of the *Phoenix* article. It was one of many which dropped onto the mat during that nightmare. I had taken a copy of the letter and sent back the original to him. I destroyed all the other letters I received. Although I hated and feared Williams the same as all other journalists, the letter appeared to be sympathetic and understanding. But I could trust no one.

One afternoon I got a call from Peter Lennon in relation to other legal moves he was making about the will. He told me that he had sought advice from a friend about the prospect of going public with a story like ours. The friend had suggested that Paul Williams could be trusted with the story. He was also the ideal candidate to help me write a book on my life because he had almost completed another book on the criminal, the General. I was flabbergasted at the coincidence and agreed that Peter should contact him. Peter drew up a confidentiality agreement in case I decided to change my mind.

A few weeks later Peter again rang and told me he had met with Paul Williams. He said that he was suitably impressed and reckoned he was the right man for the job. He had done quite a bit of research into our story and knew a lot more than I thought the media knew. He was very interested and sympathetic and agreed to undertake the story. There were further consultations between Peter Lennon, Paul Williams and the editor of the *Sunday World*, Colm MacGinty. Before a meeting was arranged to meet with Ross and myself, both of them conducted their own investigations into my claims. They were also given full access to all the documentation, letters and pictures I had.

The day we went to meet with them for the first time, both Ross and I were terrified. They were the kind of people we had lived in fear of, the people Michael said never to trust. They were the people we would go to another planet to avoid. Now we would find ourselves sitting across a table from them. Just before we left to take the bus Ross stopped in the door, the apprehension was written all over his face. 'Mum, do you think we're doing the right thing?' 'I don't know, Ross,' I said, rubbing his head. 'We will never know that. All I know is that we have to do something because nothing is happening. It is the only way I can see us getting out of this hell.' Ross smiled. He needed reassurance.

We were sitting around a conference table in Peter's office when he introduced Colm MacGinty and Paul Williams. I had expected two brash, obnoxious newsmen. Deep down I felt that I wouldn't like them and we would decide not to go ahead. Instead they were reassuring, courteous and friendly. Professionals with a human touch. I suddenly felt at ease with them and the knot in my stomach loosened somewhat. They had done their homework and put forward their proposals for how to deal with the story which they were totally happy with. There were a lot of questions and clarifications. After that, Paul began interviewing both of us at length. Both he and Colm MacGinty have been very supportive to Ross and me since then.

In the weeks and months leading up to the story it was kept a closely guarded secret, known only to a handful of people. I have since heard people saying that it was one of the best-kept secrets in the media. As the print date approached, 25 June, Ross and I were very nervous. We knew the storm which our story would create and the amount of abuse and allegations we would have to face. But anything was better than what we had been through. Deep down I began to feel a sense of optimism that the journey was almost over. It was one of the most marvellous summers this country has seen for many years and that also boosted our morale. The morning before the publication date the *Sunday World* took us out of town. It was one of the things we requested. We knew that there would be a media frenzy when the story appeared.

Now, three months after we told our story to the world, the controversy has abated somewhat. It has been a hard time but at least now our son can hold his head up and no longer be confused or angry about who he is. Now I hope and pray to God that we can get on with the rest of our lives with a degree of peace and happiness. We can only now grieve for the man we both loved and adored since the smothering cloak of secrecy has been lifted off us.

A lot of people will say that my life with Michael Cleary was a mess. Perhaps they're right. Both of us were reckless, immature and naïve. The joy and happiness was more than adequately balanced against much pain and despair. I will never know if I made a mistake when I fell in love with that wonderful man and priest. There are times when I feel anger at Michael that he left us this way. I made three attempts to leave the relationship but the enduring love between us, and the hand of fate, brought us back to each other's arms. But I am left with a lot of questions the answers to which I will never know. Did Michael's need to have me around him all the time stem from a fear that somehow if we were apart, his secret would become known? Did he just like controlling me? Was I merely his property? Deep down my heart tells that that was a small part of it but his main motivation was love. A love he felt guilty about.

Few of us ever chart out our lives, I certainly didn't. My life and emotions are scattered to the four winds. I must accept that this was part of God's plan for me. Now all I can look to is tomorrow and the hope that Ross and I can start a new life free from the shackles of secrecy and fear. I have told our story. Now it is time to move on and live the rest of the life I have left on this planet. I pray that my son will find his way and be happy. When I have achieved that I don't mind dying because I know that one day I will be with them both in a happier, eternal place.